THE ONLINE MONEY BOOK

BY

STEPHEN AKINTAYO

ABOUT THE AUTHOR

Stephen Akintayo is a Nigerian author and Digital Marketing Consultant, Entrepreneur, Business/Relationship Coach, TV/Radio Host, and Philanthropist. He is currently the MD/CEO of Gtext Group, a leading firm in Nigeria whose services span from digital marketing, website design, bulk SMS, and online advertising, to media, e-commerce, real estate, consulting, and a host of other services.

He was born in Gonge Area of Maiduguri, Borno State, Nigeria to Mr. Victor and Mrs. Deborah Akintayo, in an impoverished environment with no electricity or potable drinking water. After his father's business crumbled, feeding became the biggest challenge of his family - whilst in primary school, he scavenged for his lunch. His passion for philanthropy was birthed by his humble beginnings. In his words; "My surname was poverty. Hunger was my biggest challenge."

Stephen spent the first twelve years of his life living in the forest of Maiduguri (along Danboa road). The living conditions were so bad that he slept on a mattress for the first time at the age of 13. As a result of the family's struggles, his primary school education was spotty.

Things got better in secondary school, though his mum had to borrow money each term to pay his school fees. His future looked very bleak. At 16, he read his first business book, Rich Dad Poor Dad, and that propelled him to his achievements. He started the business a year later, selling GNLD food supplements (introduced to him by his cousin).

Not long after, he ventured into his first online business, selling eBooks he bought for $10. From there, he did a dozen more businesses with varying degrees of success. His major inspiration for doing business was his mother. He wanted to succeed to compensate a very hard-working mother who denied herself everything in order to educate her 5 children.

A day before hosting one of his most successful Student Trade Fairs, his mother died of ovarian cancer! This was the toughest season of his life and business career.

Stephen Akintayo's story is indeed a grass to grace one. His singular regret in life is that his hard-working mother died before she could witness some of the good works God is doing through him today.

One of the companies he founded, Gilead Balm Group Services, has assisted a number of businesses in Nigeria to move to enviable levels by helping them reach their clients through its enormous nationwide database of real phone numbers and email addresses.

It has hundreds of organizations as its clients including multinational companies like Guaranty Bank, PZ Cussons, MTN, Chivita, amongst others.

He is also the Founder and President of Infinity Foundation and Stephen Akintayo Foundation, indigenous non-governmental organizations that assist orphans and vulnerable children as well as mentor young minds.

The foundation has assisted over 2,000 orphans and vulnerable children and has also partnered with 22 orphanage homes in the country.

In December 2015 he started Mercy Orphanage through Infinity Foundation to care for victims of Boko Haram insurgence in the Northern part of Nigeria.

Stephen Akintayo Foundation focuses on Financial Grants with an initial grant of $2,500 to 20 entrepreneurs in 2015, and plans to grow that to $1.4m annual grant by the 5th year; projects like Upgrade Conference and The Serial Entrepreneur Conference with thousands of attendees who benefit from high-value knowledge from exceptional speakers and consultants.

Stephen is also the founder of Omonaija, an online radio station in Lagos currently streaming 24 hours daily. His first degree is in Microbiology from Olabisi Onabanjo University.

He is a member of the Institute of Strategic Management and a professional member of the Institute of Information Management.

An ordained Pastor with Living Faith Church Worldwide, he is happily married to Mrs. Olabisi Akintayo and blessed with African children.

To invite Stephen Akintayo for a speaking engagement kindly email: info@stephenakintayo.com or call: 08180000618.

IMPORTANT LEGAL STUFF

Table of Contents

Section 4: Additional Video Ads Tips to consider

Introduction

Welcome to the latest and very easy to apply The Online Money Book Training, designed to take you by the hand and walk you through the process of making some good money over the web. I'm very excited to have you here, and I know this will be very helpful for you.

This exclusive training will show you step-by-step, topic by topic, and tool by tool, what you need to know to dominate making money online in the easiest way possible, using the most effective tools and in the shortest time ever. This training comprises 15 premium chapters organized into 4 sections.

This is exactly what you are going to learn:

Section 1: Basics of Making Money Online.

In Chapter One through to Four, we will talk about: What making money online is all about? Why you should make money online, what are the most common ways to make money online? And What you need to make money online?

Section 2: Easy Ways to Make Money Online

In Chapter Five through to Seven, we will talk about: Making Easy Money Online by Taking Survey

Section 3: Advanced Ways to Make Money Online

In Chapter Eight through to Twelve, we will talk about: Blogging, Freelancing, Email Marketing and Webinar Marketing

Section 4: Additional Tips to consider

In Chapter Thirteen through to Sixteen, we will talk about: Do's to apply, Don'ts to avoid.

Well, it is time for you to start making some good money online.

SECTION 1

Basics of Making Money Online

CHAPTER ONE

WHAT IS MAKING MONEY ONLINE ALL ABOUT

Apparently, money has become the basics for all deeds in our world today, and human beings have found a lot of ways to earn these dollars and pound notes for themselves.

One of the ways to make money, where you won't have to invest huge amounts of it, is through the biggest revelation of this century - the Internet.

With the horizons of the internet spreading far and wide, the ways in which you can earn money have become plenty.

What making money online really means

One of the major concepts to comprehend how to make money online is learning the deep meaning of the subject. Making money online is a very wide concept and it is a young industry with not many people comprehending it. Once you comprehend a concept, you'll succeed in that area.

Understanding what it is will assist you become a successful marketer and entrepreneur.

Making money online can portray a variety of things. It can be as simple as filling out surveys for points on a site which converts into real life items. Out of this variety of jobs, one thing is usual; the output of your input is money or something of value.

Can you make money online as a service provider?

The rewards of the internet goes beyond searching for details needed for any desired topic. People remain in touch with each other through social media sites, and countless businesses rely on the web to succeed.

Most manufacturers and service providers can be reached through the net. The internet has facilitated quick and efficient communications while offering many channels for entertainment. Apart from this well-known benefits, the net is also being exploited for making money online.

Many professionals claim to survive with the money generated through online sources. Students are also making money through the net. In fact, there are hundreds of ways to make money by working online.

Money can be made online through the rendering of services like article writing, affiliate marketing, owning a website or blog, and becoming a virtual assistant for an online company. Through these services, dollars can be made online.

However, making money has never been easy, and that remains valid for online money as well. One also needs to be aware of the different available opportunities for making money through the internet and recognize the most suitable one.

Can you earn money online as a business owner or entrepreneur?

Another way for online money making includes your knowledge of business. The internet is the most efficient and simple way of buying and selling when owning a store at online marketplaces like Amazon, eBay, Fiverr and so on.

eBay is very popular today, and it is one of the largest marketplaces online. On eBay, you can not only buy, but also sell. You can use this site for buying things at lower prices and selling them for higher prices to earn profits.

With online sales continuously on the rise, selling products to web shoppers is a great path to follow for business purposes.

Can you make money online as a regular online user?

Being a regular online user creates an avenue for your knowledge to make you money through the use of the internet.

Money can be made through provisions of professional and specialized observations based on your area of expertise.

Here, you can decide whether you want to work solely online, or combine face-to-face services with your digital ones.

CHAPTER TWO

WHY YOU SHOULD MAKE MONEY ONLINE

Internet technology has transformed our lives forever. It has opened up unlimited opportunities to market our products, services, and informations. Also, it has become the new frontier for finding ways to make money.

We live in a world where the economy is often a little unsettled to say the least, and unemployment is soaring in many areas.This is all the more reason why you should think about part-time online income from home.

Great Benefits

Even if you have a full-time job, making money online can be an extra income option. There are many reasons why you should be making money online.

Work from Home

There is nothing that feels so good like working from home. You can avoid too much traffic each morning while not wasting money on gas. Plus, not having to set the alarm is a good feeling as well.

Making your own hours enables you to go to work whenever you feel. This means you can go out with friends on a weeknight without feeling too tired the next day.

People who know you will be jealous of the fact that your commute is nothing more than going downstairs after you wake up.

Online Revenue Can Be Passive

You don't have to put in any work to see results, inevitably. Writers can post an article once and get paid for the rest of their lives. Bloggers can get paid through advertising revenue. Generating this passive revenue means you don't have to work for your money.

You could pay for a vacation, send your kids to college or retire early thanks to this new revenue source.

Freedom to Work anywhere at any given time

This is the first and most important thing to consider when the idea to start earning money from the internet comes to your mind. The ability to take your work with you anywhere matters a lot because you will be able to meet deadlines and please your customers.

The freedom for you to work anywhere also makes the work fun and less stressful rather than sitting in an office in one particular spot over-working yourself.

Deal With Whomever You Want

You can decide who you want to work with when you work online. Picking your clients enables you to develop relationships with people who share your vision. Work is a lot more fun when you are working on things that matter to you.

Writing about your favorite cause is more fun than spending your day ringing up groceries.

Also, not having a boss to contend with is a huge relief. Most online work is either freelance or independent contractor work.

Enlarge your horizons

For most people, making money online and working from home is a brand-new field. There is so much to learn, and as your knowledge grows your income increases. I remember some people saying that making money online drove them to learn more about the internet and marketing.

From simple PTC to running their own site, and from Google adsense to selling Clickbank products, it involves so many things that if only people would learn more, they could make more from the internet.

A way of entertainment

Some people only see making money online as a way of relaxing and entertaining themselves. To them, it is like browsing youtube videos and reading articles. To be honest with you, almost everything you do on the internet can make you money; such as forum posting, video uploading, writing articles, searching, sharing files, surfing, etc.

Strengthen your feeling of achievement

If you get your first reward, it will encourage you to learn more. You can achieve your goal if you are encouraged. Since making online income is not as simple as it sounds, it is not something everyone can achieve. If you are already making money from your online activities, you are one step ahead of the pack.

Use Your Business Plans

Use your business experience to do things your way. No one is going to tell you that your marketing plan won't work.

Nobody is going to stop you from pursuing a project because of office politics. You can expand into new markets; attract new clients and create your own company culture.

Running your own online business will help you hone your leadership skills without being sued for making mistakes.

Surprising Facts and Figures

- ✓ There are 4,596,319,087 Internet Users in the world today.
- ✓ There are 1,779,840, 042 Total number of Websites today.
- ✓ Digital interactions influenced retail sales to the tune of $2.2 trillion in 2015.
- ✓ 40% of global internet users have bought products or goods online.
- ✓ A single second of delay in your website loading time can result in a 7% loss in conversion and 40% of web users will leave a website if it takes longer than 3 seconds to load.
- ✓ Worldwide B2C e-commerce sales reached $1.7 trillion in 2015, and it is estimated to reach $2.35 trillion by 2018.
- ✓ 8 out of 10 consumers will shop online if offered free shipping.
- ✓ Personalized recommendations can increase conversion rates by up to 5.5 times.
- ✓ An increase in site speed from 8 to 2 seconds can boost your conversion rate by 74%.

✓ E-commerce sales from social media grew by 202% in 2014 and is expected to further increase.

✓ Mobile advertising spend is projected to account for 60.4% of all digital advertising spend by 2016 and 72.2% of all digital advertising spend by 2019.

✓ Spending on digital marketing is projected to increase by 12% to 15% on average. Social media's share of the total marketing budget will grow from 10% in 2015 to 14% this year, while spending on offline advertising will fall 2%.

✓ After SEM, online display advertising (banner ads and retargeting) capture the biggest share of online spending at 34%, representing roughly 10% of total marketing budgets.

✓ The average person now spends more time online than with TV and all other media (newspapers, magazines, etc.) combined.

CHAPTER THREE

WHAT ARE THE MOST COMMON WAYS TO MAKE MONEY ONLINE

There are millions of ways to make money online. The opportunities on the web are endless, yet most people find it very hard to make money online.

This has led to a belief in a growing number of people who think it is just too hard to make money online from home. The reality is that it can be easy to make money online if you know how, and are willing to put in the work. The first step to make money online is self-explanatory.

Starting a Blog

Blogging mainly consists of writing posts, publishing posts and maintaining the blog. One of the most reliable ways to make passive income online is to create a website or blog.

You may have to invest in a web host if you get serious about this, but there are some free hosting sites that will enable you to use this money-making opportunity as well. To make money from advertising, your visitors have to press on one of the advertising links.

In addition to ad revenue, you can advertise on your site with affiliate partners who will pay you when one of your visitors clicks on the link and signs up for the advertiser's services. You will only get paid by the affiliate if a transaction is done.

Taking surveys

There are sites that can aid you make money anywhere from pocket change to a full income. These are free to join, paid survey sites where you take surveys for a small payback. If you get other members to join under you, then you will get a percentage of their earnings too. This is how you make genuine money. Some people have reported verifiable earnings of around $1,800 per month this way.

Downloading and installing apps

A lot of companies, including Google, pay you for installing their apps. Moreover, you get paid for each month the apps are installed on your phone. Some of these sites include: ShopTracker and MobileXpression.

Review stuff

You can turn this into an opportunity to earn an income, and one way to do it would be by writing reviews for various products and getting paid for it. Posting and writing a review can earn you anywhere between $5 and $50 per review, based on the necessities. Yelp and ReviewMe can give you some special invites.

Testing websites

This involves visiting a particular website and performing an exact function on the website. While you are performing the task, your screen is being recorded to track your mouse movement and clicks. Also, your voice is recorded as you verbalize your steps on the website. You can earn about $10 for about 10 to 20 minutes of website testing.

Signing up for gift cards

This implies earning free cash & gift cards for things you do online everyday. eBay gives you a $10 gift card when you sign up and earn your first cashback refund. It's great for online shoppers. You can redeem your points for gift cards to your favorite stores, such as Amazon.com and Walmart, or redeem your points for cash through PayPal. It's simple and fun!

Get paid for being healthy

Being healthy already has so many rewards, but you can also get paid for being healthy. The health app achievement gives you points for being healthy and doing things like walking, tracking your food, or taking health surveys.

You can earn points which can be redeemed for cash or Amazon Gift Cards. For every 10,000 points, you earn $10, and there is no limit to your earnings.

Become a freelancer

Freelancing is a time-honoured way for writers and graphic designers to make money. It's not uncommon for administrative assistants, accountants, computer programmers and other professionals to also find freelance opportunities. Look at niche job sites such as Upwork, Guru, and Fiverr.

If you're a super-speedy typist, have a good ear and write well, you might be cut out for transcription work. Transcribers provide closed captioning for films and TV shows, and written transcripts of academic presentations and focus groups.

Virtual assistant

A virtual assistant is self-employed and provides professional administrative or technical assistance to clients remotely from a home office.

Becoming a Virtual Assistant can be a tremendous experience if you have strong administrative skills, organized, capable of working with deadlines and would like to run a business from home.

Virtual Assistances (VAs) can do everything from checking emails and making travel plans to handling internet research or working for their small business.

High-end earners can command $30-$100 an hour. Some reputable sites for virtual assistants are Zirtual and Upwork.

Tutoring

Tutoring services is a centralized academic online support service comprising of peer facilitated learning experiences for undergraduates interested in requesting or becoming a tutor for students. Select your schedule if you have some imperative routine tasks or go for online tutoring and earn $20 per hour on Chegg Tutors.

Work for Amazon

Have you heard of Amazon Mechanical Turk? Unlike other online sites that look for contract aid, the Amazon Mechanical Turk service offers simple tasks that can be done by almost anyone with a laptop. These are services that requires human interaction. You can work from home, have flexible hours and get paid by one of the world's largest retailers.

Selling lesson plans

This includes the online selling of your lesson plans particularly to new teachers. Teachers-Pay-Teachers is a marketplace for educators where you can sell and share your teaching resources.

Maintaining social media accounts

There are plenty money making opportunities on social media than you might have discovered. Maintaining social media accounts like Facebook, Twitter, and LinkedIn, in fact, can be very lucrative and high paying.

Maintaining fan pages

Facebook pages are the biggest source of earning money online. You can rapidly earn with Facebook fan pages, likes & groups. You can also sell products there for earning money as an affiliate marketer. Moreover, you can earn money by promoting other people's products on your page.

Selling An Ebook

If you enjoy writing, then publishing your eBook can be a tremendous way to earn money. The marketing of eBooks generates more online sales. Web sites like Amazon, Barnes & Noble, and Kobo all have self-publishing services, which means getting your eBook published isn't as hard as you might think. In fact, it's fairly easy.

Selling Audiobooks

It's no secret that downloadable audiobook sales have exploded on the web. Audiobooks could overtake printed books as a top selling product line on the web. Selling Audiobooks is lucrative because you can earn $50 - $500 per month.

Selling Apps

Selling an app has never been any easier. Start an app auction for $9 with Flippa, and reach out to a niche audience of motivated international app buyers in minutes. Selling apps online can earn you money monthly.

Selling your Stuff

These days, there are plenty of free online marketplaces available, and an online forum isn't all that difficult to start. Once you've managed to get an active community together, you can easily start earning money by selling your stuff and the workload isn't all that great.

Working for "Work At Home" Companies

Many online companies accept virtual call center agents, call centre managers and human resource professionals to work at home, as well as a few Tech jobs.

Virtual call centre agents, the largest segment of home-based workers, are employees and may work full time or part time for an hourly wage. Amazon's home-based workers are always employed during seasonal holidays.

CHAPTER FOUR

WHAT DO YOU NEED TO MAKE MONEY ONLINE

To make things easy, there are 4 different things you need to have ready in order to make money online: A product or service, online presence, a payment processor, and advertising.

Product or Service

A business must have a product or service to offer. What the product or service will be is very important, so take some time to choose wisely.

There are some products or services, like writing skills or selling products, that are more easily marketable over the internet than others. If you do not have a product of your own but want to engage in business online, one commendable idea is to enlist in an affiliate program.

By affiliating with other companies, you become an associate of an established online merchandiser, and you market their products in return for a commission. You can earn quite good money doing this. Thousands of internet marketers are flourishing by doing affiliate marketing. It's a good way to be introduced to the world of e-commerce without needing to make a significant investment in resources.

Creating an Online Presence

A website or a blog - All businesses, no matter how small, should have a website. It can be extremely basic, but it should contain the fundamental details your clients require.

You can't do without a website if your plans include selling products and services online. Your website will act as your online store. It is where potential customers can view photos of your stuff, read descriptions and ask questions regarding the products.

Social media is an important part of your online presence that improves your chances of generating additional revenue and building customer loyalty.

It enables customers, potential customers, and other interested parties, to engage easily via a channel that plays an important role in their everyday lives.

Notwithstanding, not every social media channel will be important to each business, it's worth looking into your options. For instance, Facebook, Twitter, Instagram, Google+, LinkedIn, YouTube, Pinterest, and Tumblr will serve a purpose for almost any business.

Creating an email account is an inexpensive, yet effective option. It is a tremendous way to build your brand and look more professional to the outside world.

Using a company-branded email address like yourname@yourcompany.com goes well. 80% of consumers surveyed said they would trust a company-branded email address more so than a free email address.

Payment Processor

PayPal is the world's most popularly used payment system. PayPal payments are made using a user's existing account or with a credit card.

Money can be sent straight to an email address, thus prompting the users to sign up for a new PayPal account. In addition to taking payments, PayPal also enables its users to send money through the service, which is a feature that only a few payment solutions provide.

Google Checkout is Google's answer to PayPal. Google Checkout enables users to pay for goods and services through an account connected to their Google profile.

The major reward that Google Checkout has over the competition is that millions of Internet users use Google for other services, making a purchase through Checkout as a simpler process.

WePay is a payment processor that enables internet merchants to accept credit cards and bank account payments online. WePay seems to be focused on the individual user and has recently added e-store pages to their service to aid their customers conveniently take payments through their service.

Advertising

Advertising is simply about getting your business in front of a potential clients who are interested in your product or service. Today, more small organizations are coming online to increase sales, gain support, and reach a rapidly growing market.

There are some different ways in which a website can get itself advertised on the web. There are contextual ads on search engine results in pages, banner ads, Rich Media Ads, Social network advertising, online classified advertising, integrating pop-ups on a visited site, advertising networks, and email marketing, including email spam.

SECTION 2

Easy Ways to Make Money Online

CHAPTER FIVE

MAKING EASY MONEY ONLINE BY TAKING SURVEYS

Surveys are an excellent tool for searching important details directly from a wide audience, with ease and convenience. Companies/Organizations often use surveys to gain a deeper comprehension of their customers' tastes and opinions.

For a few minutes of form filling, you can make a couple of points which is paid as cash or rewards. You can bag up to £3 ($5) for some surveys at websites like:

Surverjunke.com

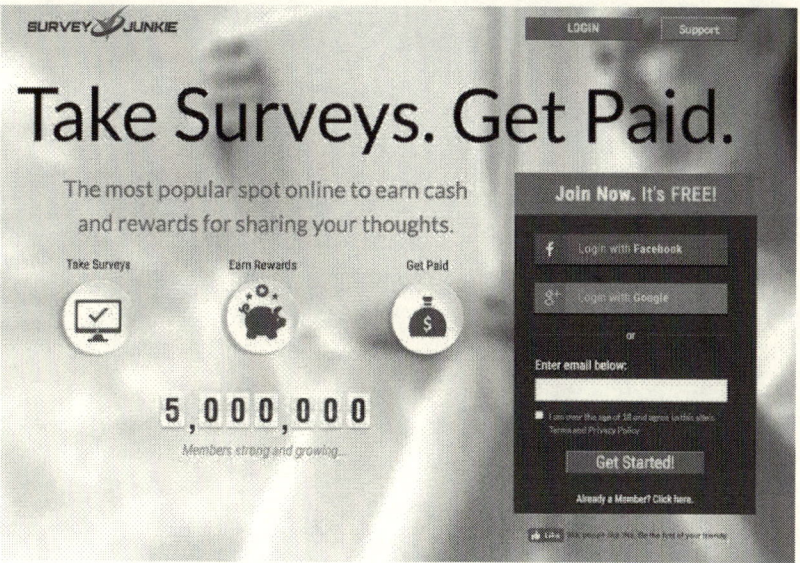

Survey Junkie, situated online at SurveyJunkie.com, is a website which gives their members the ability to take part in various forms of market research through a variety of companies to earn money from home.

Their website says that, with them, you can receive surveys earning between $2 and $75 each, as well as get involved in focus groups at up to $120 an hour, and evaluate new products in trials which allow you to keep the products for free.

Swagbucks.com

Swagbucks is the web's leading rewards program that gives its over 19 million members gift cards for their everyday online activities like taking a survey. Earn points when you shop at your favorite retailers, watch entertaining videos, search the web, answer surveys and find great deals.

Oneopinion.com

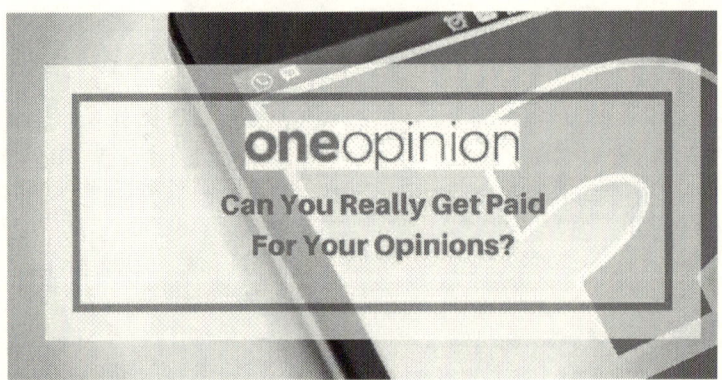

OneOpinion is a fun and simple paid survey site, rewarding you for sharing your opinion with leading market research companies. OneOpinion pays through PayPal for each survey.

Acop.com

American Consumer Opinion, found at acop.com, is a survey panel created by Decision Analyst. Membership in American Consumer Opinion® is free. You'll never have to pay any money to be a member. Incentives at ACOP range in value from 100 to 5,000 Points per survey or research project, depending on the time it takes. A point equals a penny.

Pineconeresearch.com

Pine Cone Research is a trusted leader in gathering the opinions of consumers nationwide. Pinecone research is one of the best websites for paid surveys. Pinecone Research pays members $3 per survey with no disqualifications, but getting in isn't always simple. Learn why Pinecone makes it hard to get in, and why it is worth trying.

Paidsurveys.com

PaidSurveys is a 100% free survey site connecting you with top market research companies that need to hear your opinion. For taking a survey at PaidSurvey.com, you can earn up to £300 per month, paid directly into your PayPal account.

OpinionOutpost.com

Opinion Outpost Surveys, found at opinionoutpost.com, is a marketing research and survey company where you can make little money by sharing your opinions on products and services by filling out surveys.

By taking Opinion Outpost surveys, you gain points, and the basic point structure is 10 "points" for one-dollar in the United States. You get more points for doing more surveys, and you must gain 50 points ($5) to get paid.

YouGov.com

YouGov is the authoritative measure of public opinion and consumer behavior. Each survey you take will give you a profit between £0.50 and £3.00 depending on the content. As a bonus, you get £1.00 just for signing up. The minimum payout is £50.

ProductReportCard.com

Product Report Card

Is this surveys site legit?

Product Report Card is a site that enables you to sign up to receive paid survey invitations via email. It takes less than five minutes to sign up, and it's 100% free. The money you can earn from setting up your profiles at ProductReportCard ranges from 25¢ to $5.00.

Cashcrate.com

Cash Crate is recognized as a free site that will get you paid. Advertisers work with Cash Crate to give them with individuals to test out new services and products using simple online surveys.

At Cash Crate, you're going to get paid for any of your opinion you share. It does not get any easier than that to make money online. Once you earn up to $20, you'll receive your payment in the next 30 days.

Vindale.com

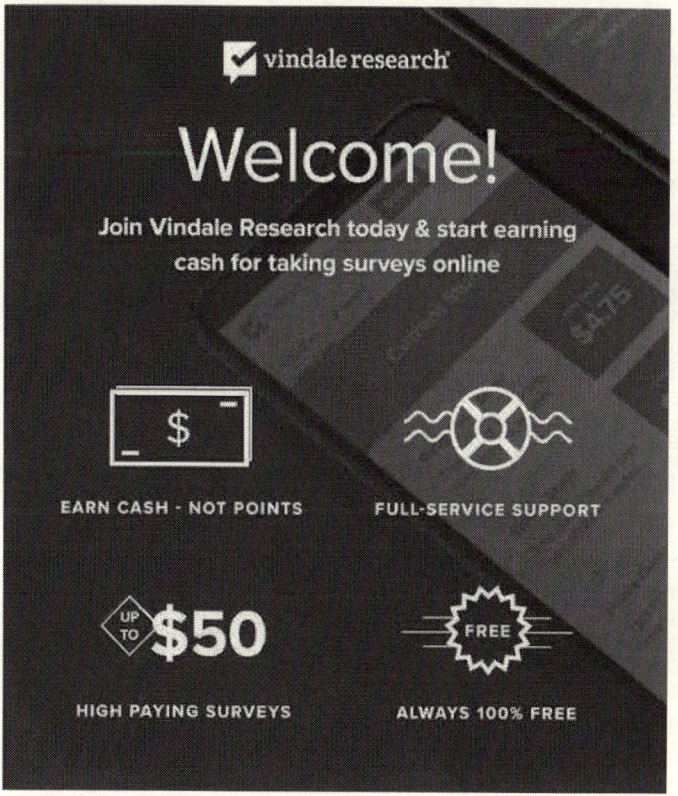

Vindale Research is an online company that takes an interesting approach to market research and online surveys, and the membership is 100% free. They advertise payouts of $5 - $75, a rate considerably higher than most competitors and state that customers will be evaluating products and services.

SurveyQueen.com

SurveyQueen is a fast, cool, and smart way for you to get paid for sharing your opinion. Surveys are paying up to $75. Join Earning Station today and start earning rewards by taking surveys and completing offers.

CHAPTER SIX

MAKING EASY MONEY ONLINE BY TESTING STUFF

Over the years, product testing has been one of the most genuine ways to make money from home. There are many benefits of working from home, including not having to commute, working on your schedule and so much more.

There are a variety of ways to make money from home with one of them being testing free products. Some companies will send you sample products, while others will send full sized ones, which you will test every month and then pay you for giving them your thoughts on the products. These online testing companies include:

Usertesting.com

UserTesting.com is a website that hires regular Internet users to test websites and record their experiences. UserTesting pays $10 via PayPal for every 20-minute video you complete to visit websites or apps, complete a set of tasks, and make your thoughts clear.

Enrollapp.com

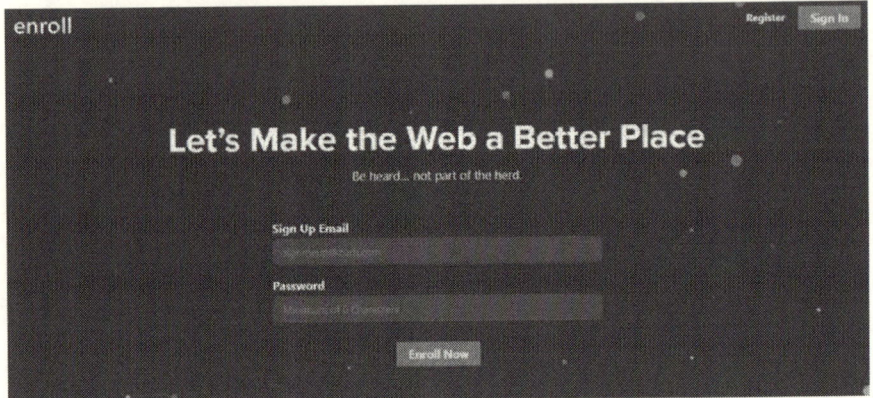

Enrollapp is a firm that fits into a bit of a cliché phrase; making the web a better place for everyone. Enrollapp was created to help developers see what users expect from a website in certain niches. Enrollapp pays a certain amount of money for every test you perform. On their website, you can launch a demo test and get paid via PayPal once your balance reaches just $1.

Testingtime.com

Testing Time is open to global residents that hire and pay individuals to test digital products via Skype. You can earn up to €50 per study.

Each study is conducted via Skype and usually takes 30 – 90 minutes of time. Once the study is completed, you'll get paid within 5 – 10 days via PayPal.

Testbirds.com

Testbirds is a company that pays you to test software like websites, apps, games, etc. before they are released. On average, you are paid around 10 euros for every hour that you are testing, as well as around 1 to 5 euros for each bug you find while testing.

Trymyui.com

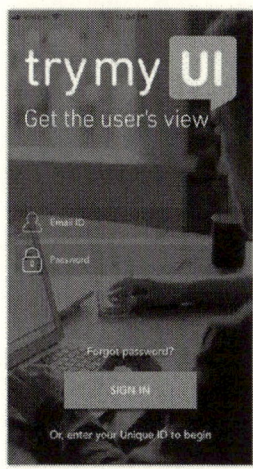 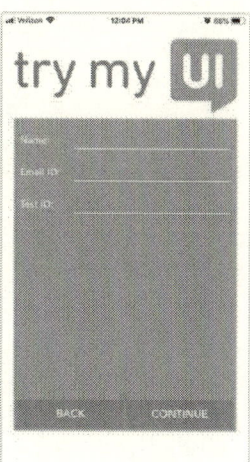

TryMyUi keeps it easy. You get paid for a website or app test. Earn $10 for 15 –20 minutes of your time and payments are made bi-weekly via PayPal. To be part of the TryMyUI team, sign up for an account.

Userlytics

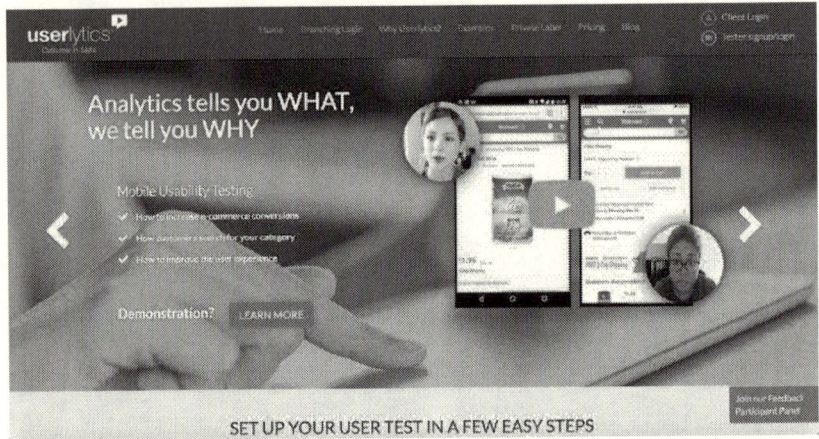

Userlytics is a website that pays you for giving feedback on websites, applications, prototypes, concepts and more. To apply, register for an account, and then wait for an invite to complete an assignment. Once you've finished your assignment, you'll be paid $10 per task via PayPal.

Userfeel.com

Userfeel.com is a test website that enables you to talk about your thoughts on different websites. You get paid $10 for the task on websites. To become a website tester, register for an account, and take a sample test.

Once your sample is approved, you'll start getting assignments by email. Good testers can earn $100-$200 per week and Payments are made via PayPal at the end of each week.

Validately.com

Validately hires testers to complete mobile and website tests for companies. At the completion of a 5-minute test, you'll get paid $5.

Live tests where you speak via phone and share a screen with a moderator, pay a minimum of $25 for 30 minutes. Payments are made via PayPal within five business days of the test.

WhatUsersDo.com

WhatUsersDo.com is an Internet-based usability testing and website review service that pays to give feedback on clients' websites. After you've been approved, you'll receive assignments via email. Each test takes about 20 minutes to complete and pays £8, or around $12.50. Payments are made via PayPal on the 25th day of each month.

UserZoom.com

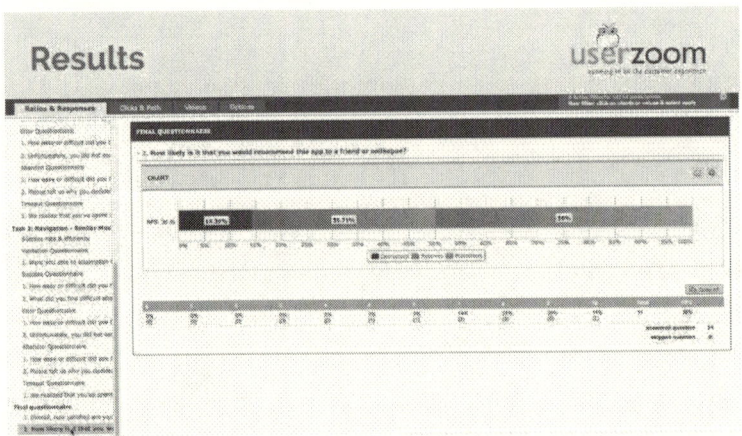

UserZoom is a company that conducts website usability tests for desktop and mobile platforms. Tests pay an average of $5 to $10 depending on the complexity of the study. Most tests take between 10 and 20 minutes to complete, and payments are made via PayPal 10 to 14 business days after the completion of the study.

BetaFamily.com

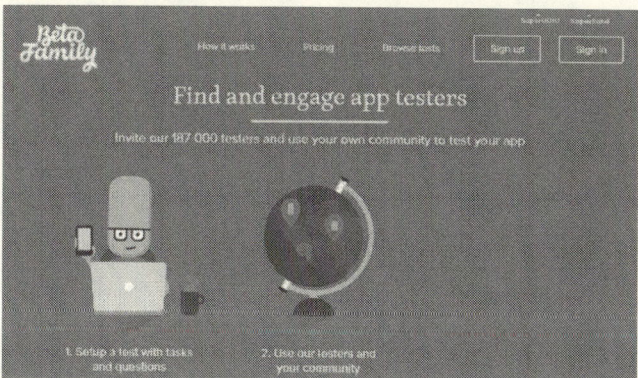

Beta Family is a crowd testing community for beta testing of iOS and Android applications. BetaFamily pays once you earn above $50, and the payment is processed within 30 days.

CHAPTER SEVEN

MAKING EASY MONEY ONLINE BY PERFORMING EASY TASKS

Making money by doing simple online tasks is now easy with the increase of people seeking help through the internet. The tasks that need to be done are quite simple.

A short task is any job or assignment that can be done in a short amount of time. The tasks that can be completed vary greatly in nature, as does the pay. The reason this is such a great opportunity for moms is that, the tasks can be concluded at any time, and the majority of short tasks don't require moms to be on the phone, which requires a quiet household.

MTurk.com

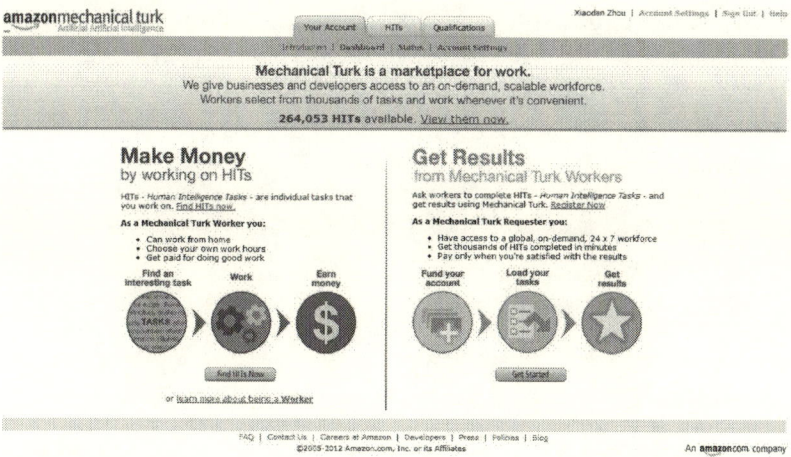

Mechanical Turk is a web service that provides an on-demand, scalable, human workforce to complete jobs that humans can do better than computers, for instance recognizing objects in photos. MTurk workers earn somewhere between $3 and $3.25 per hour of work.

Viggle

Viggle is a loyalty program for television that gives people real rewards fo checking into the television shows they're watching. Recently available for Apple iPhone, iPad and iPod touch, Viggle instantly identifies wha television shows users are watching and awards them points when they check-in. Viggle users can redeem their points in the app's rewards catalog for items such as movie tickets, music, & gift cards.

Fronto.co

Fronto is the world's first mobile lock screen media, which shows curate arties, hot new apps, deals and promos to mobile users through the everyday lock screen in a really seamless way.

By simply waking up your phone, you can read trending articles, earn rewards, download coupons, and learn about new promotional deals. Fronto offers Amazon.com Gift Card or Paypal payout. You just go to 'Redeem Gift Card Shop' to buy an Amazon.com Gift Card.

Cosign.co

CoSign is the first app to make products in your photos available to buy, turning your social media followers into customers and your style into a way to earn cash rewards.

CoSign is the best way to earn rewards for sharing your style with friends and followers. You get cash each time a follower shops directly from your photos.

Use the COSIGN app to track image earnings and cash out at your convenience.

ADMimsy.com

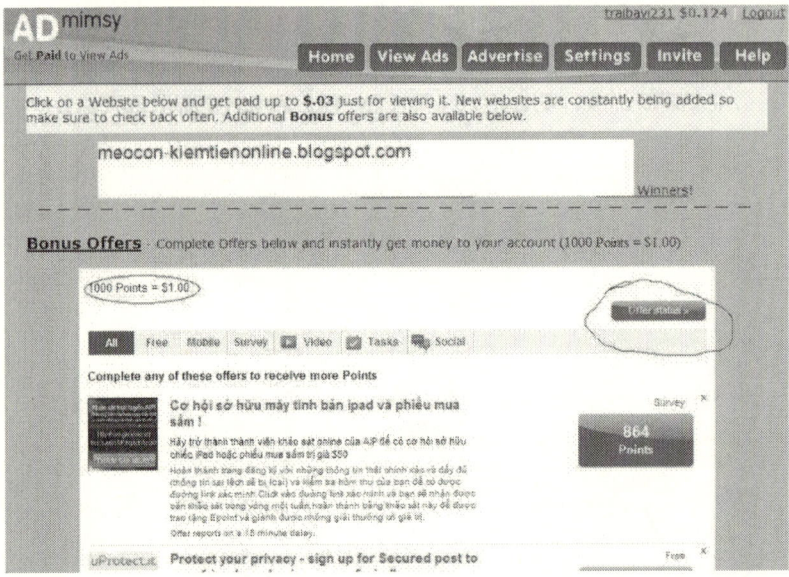

ADmimsy is a site for earning money online. Money is made via the viewing of Ads, and you'll get paid up to $.02 per Ad view. You also get paid up to $.01 for every Ad your referrals view.

MobeeApp.com

The Mobee App is an app that you can download to your iPhone or Android to get paid to mystery shop, by basically performing the simple task of just eating out and giving feedback. Mobee is a first of its kind app that pays you to do these tasks.

It turns just about anyone with an iPhone or Android into a mystery shopper, who can earn money or rewards. Each 100 point "mission" translates to $1, and there is no limit to the amount of missions users can claim.

Lucktastic.com

Lucktastic is an "instant-win" scratch off mobile app game in which its users have a chance to win tokens or even cash by performing a simple task depending on the offer for that specific scratch off card.

PactApp.com

Pact is one of the best ways to keep your fitness and weight loss resolutions. Earn cash for staying active. Pact will motivate you to hit your health goals week to-week by setting your exercise and healthy eating goals each week, Increase your fitness level, and informs you of your cash earnings each week.

Ibotta.com

Ibotta is an app for smartphones that has many different money saving offers for popular products. To get paid by Ibotta, you have to redeem offers totaling $5 or more, and Ibotta will let you transfer your earnings directly to your PayPal account.

ReceiptHog.com

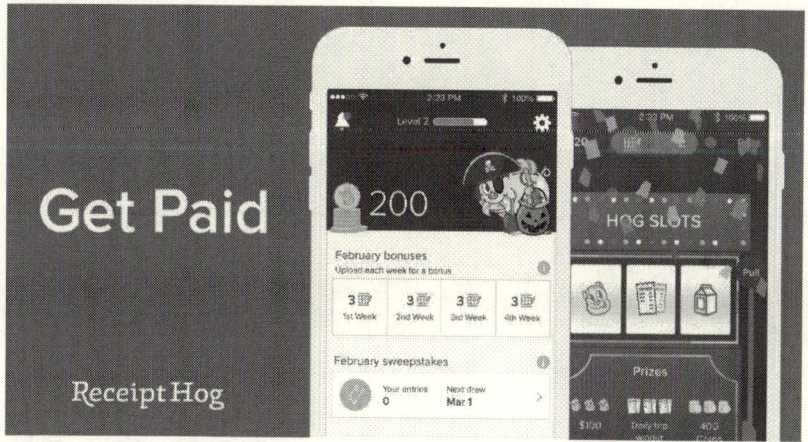

Receipt Hog is a mobile app that actually rewards users for snapping pictures of their grocery receipts. For each receipt you upload, you'll earn coins which can be redeemed for cash. Receipt Hog is very simple to use; it enables you to earn 10 coins per receipt uploaded.

SECTION 3

Advanced Ways to Make Money Online

CHAPTER EIGHT

BLOGGING

The blog is an abbreviated version of "weblog," which is a term used to depict websites that maintain an ongoing record of information. Blogging in every sense is the act of journaling online, either with a plan or without. It is the procedure by which we share or reach out and break down cultural and ideological divides.

Why You Should Blog

The number one reason why you should blog is because it creates opportunities. The most crucial reason to start a blog is that it creates alot opportunities for its owner. The opportunities could be friendship, financial gain or self-growth, blogging puts your personality out there for the world, and gets you noticed in a very unique way.

Blogging has huge financial advantages

Blogging has made a fortune for a lot of people. Someone like Linda Ikeji became a billionaire through blogging. But most top bloggers today started out not looking at the money but they were consistent and passionate about the topic or things they blogged about and their effort beared much fruit in years to come.

So whether you make $20/year or $20,000/year, it's still great. As long as you keep being consistent and committed, blogging will definitely pay you.

However, advertising on your blog can help you financially, as can accepting sponsors if you're reviewing products. Eventually, your blog can lead to a career in blogging, which may seem far off from when you began, but it's becoming far more acceptable today.

Blogging is great way to improve your writing

Blogging is one of the excellent ways to showcase your writing skills and the more you write consistently the better you get at it. Once you've created your first post, you're officially published on the Internet and can promote yourself to companies far more easily by linking your blog rather than showing outdated articles.

It enables for the potential of self-growth

Sharing stuffs with people online enables time for reflection and perspective. You'll be able to look back at past work and ideas. You can learn from them by promoting not only a form of a diary entry, but also the idea of self-growth. By placing your ideas into a public form, it gives room for your creativity to grow, as well as your confidence and ambitions.

It serves as a personal journal

Blogging serves many of the same roles as a personal journal. It trains us to be observant and gives weight to the personal growth that we are experiencing.

It prepares our minds to track life and explain the changes we are going through.

Always remember that your blog is a digital record of your life that is saved "in the cloud." In essence, it can never be lost, stolen, or destroyed in a fire.

Steps In Setting Up A Blog

- **Decide Your Reasons for Starting a Blog**

The first thing to consider is the topic you will write about in your blog. You may want to do a little bit of keyword research when deciding on a topic. If you already have a business, then your blog can easily be related to your online business. However, you can narrow your blog niche further if you wish.

- **Selecting a Blogging Platform**

This is the most daunting part of how to start a blog, because there are many blogging platforms to choose from. There are two differences when choosing a platform, and that is whether or not you want to make money from it or not.

There are sites like WordPress.com and Blogger.com which you can check out, but WordPress is by far the most popular. This is because they offer both a free platform and a self-hosted platform that is already used by millions.

- **Select a Domain Name**

Ideally, you want your topic keywords to be included in your domain name. If you have to use multiple words in your name, try to limit it to three at most. Also, try to make sure the name is very easy for people to remember.

- **Set Up Your Web Hosting**

Web hosting is connecting your domain name to the internet. You are effectively renting space on the World Wide Web and allowing people to have access to your blog.

- **Make Your First Blog Post**

Once you've set up your theme and written an About Page introducing yourself and what your blog is about, then it's time to write your first blog post. Here are some tips on how to write the perfect blog post: write eye-catching titles and headlines, use an engaging image, use proper post-segmentation, and use a call to action to each post.

How To Make Money with Blogging

There are many ways that you can make money with your blog, and you're only limited by your imagination. You should use as many ways as possible without turning your blog into a spam blog.

- **Affiliate Ads**

One of the top ways to monetize your blog is with affiliate ads. These should be Ads that are related to the content which you have on your blog, because this will ensure a higher click-through rate.

No matter what niche or market you're in, you'll always be able to find an appropriate affiliate program to promote. Other ads like Google AdSense, Yahoo Ads and Content Ads are also great ads to place on your blog.

- **Selling Stuff**

Selling stuff is another great way to make money. These could be digital products which your readers can download instantly, or they can be physical products that you'll need to ship. If you do not have your own products, you can always promote products that you are affiliated with by writing product reviews.

Another way you can obtain products is by using drop shipping. However, the amount of money you can make with drop shipping is quite small, so you may be better off by sticking with affiliate marketing.

- **Promoting Your Other Sites**

Many bloggers simply use their blogs to generate traffic and sales for their other sites. However, you want to be careful that you do not overdo the linking to one particular site. The more sites you link to, the less likely your blog will be deemed as a spam blog.

Conclusion

Blogging can really generate a stable income, but it can take a while to generate enough traffic. It is very possible to make a living from blogging. You have to be patient and determined to become a highly successful blogger.

Others have done it, and you too can. If you have a passion in an area, blog about it. You could never tell who is reading that article. If you would like to sell your skills, you can create a personal blog and market yourself. Blogging enables you to connect with clients all over the world.

CHAPTER NINE

FREELANCING

The art of working independently to earn a living while always making dedicated efforts to achieve pre-set goals is known as freelancing. A Freelancer is an individual who earns money per project. It could be short-term work or long-term project.

A freelancer is not an employee of a firm, and therefore, may be hired to complete different jobs concurrently by various individuals or firms unless contractually specified to work exclusively until a particular project is completed.

How to Begin Your Freelancing Journey

✓ Make decisions on the common freelancing jobs like writing, web design, graphic design, photography, marketing, social media management, and others.
✓ Discover your target market.
✓ Create an online portfolio.
✓ Ensure you set your prices to cover your overhead, time to do the work, as well as to earn a living.

✓ Begin by reaching out to find clients. Utilize your network to assist you connecting with potential clients.

Finding jobs as a Freelancer

fiverr.com

Fiverr is a website that enables users to post their work or "gigs" for $5.

Anything for $5! That is what Fiverr.com is all about, and there is no wonder that thousands are being added as sellers and buyers every moment. Fiverr is a huge compilation of workers offering every type of freelancing service.

Fiverr started in early 2010, and became well known that millions of users started using Fiverr to sell or buy services.

Things to know about Fiverr

✓ To create an account on Fiverr is free.
✓ List the service/product you want to sell. This listing is referred to as a 'Gig'. It contains all the details of what products or services you would like to offer, how will the buyer receive it, how many days it will you to process an order and much more.
✓ Make your Gig live and wait for your 1st order to come.

- ✓ After you receive an order, you can communicate with the buyer via Fiverr. If you want any clarification, ask the buyer. Once this is done, you have to start processing the order. Get it done and send it to the buyer.
- ✓ After the buyer receives and approves his order, your order is marked as complete, and Fiverr will credit your payment to your account.
- ✓ 14 days after your order has been marked as complete, you can withdraw the funds from your Fiverr account.

How to Make Money Using Fiverr

- ✓ Use a catchy, keyword rich title
- ✓ Immediately you have your gigs up and running and are making some decent money, you can begin to outsource your work for pennies on the dollar.

For example, set up an eBook cover design gig and have your hired help do all the work. Even after you pay your employee, you should still make a profit. This is a great way to focus on other money-making activities, such as creating new gigs.

- ✓ Find a successful gig, and offer similar services, but include a free bonus. Giving the client a guide to teach them the skills that you are providing will give the customer more bang for their buck.
- ✓ Every time you learn a new skill, offer to sell it on Fiverr. You can adjust your content depending on how much traffic you are receiving.

Freelancer.com

Freelancer is a marketplace where employers and employees can find each other. The site enables employers to post work to be done. Anyone is able to offer quotes to complete the project, after which the employer can award the work.

At Freelancer, you can make money from freelancing services, content writing, translating, graphic designing, programming and other categories, as well. Freelancer takes a 10% fee, which can be reduced with a paid monthly membership, with a minimum fee of $5. How to Make Money from Freelancer.com

The moment you sign up, you'll have an account at Freelancer. You are free to start making money online by browsing projects by category or by title. You can search the projects you are interested in, and the ones that match your experience and fields of interest.

Then, considering the employer's needs, you place your bid on different projects, depending on the minimum and maximum amount of money offered by the employer.

Making money from Freelancer can be easier when you upgrade your membership. Beyond the free membership, there is the basic one, which enables you to place 50 bids per month and select up to 30 categories of skills.

Then, there is the standard membership, giving you 150 bids monthly, with an option of 60 skills selection. The higher you upgrade your membership, the more chance you have to make money online from Freelancer.

The premium membership allows you 500 bids every month and enables you to select 100 different types of skills for your profile, which also means that your chances of being awarded projects are increased.

Guru.com

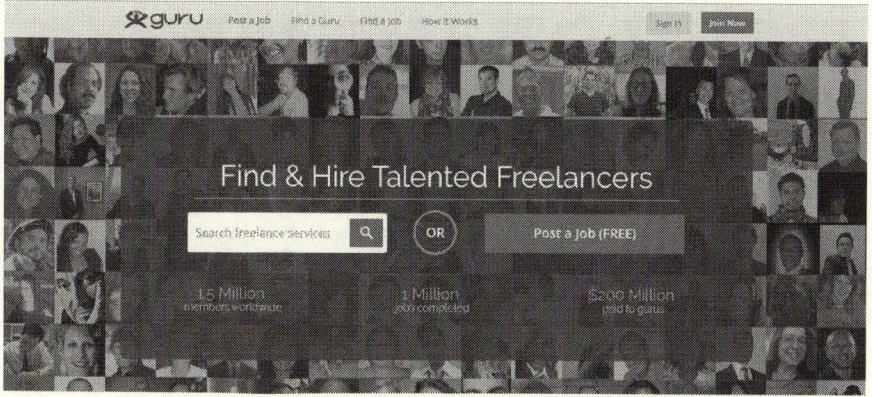

Guru operates as a platform to match up outsourced service providers with people in need of their services. Guru has over 100 categories that you can select from when submitting outsourced tasks and campaigns.

Here's how it functions

As an employer, you submit your job description and specs. Outsourcers in the category you specified read your project description and can bid on the task.

You receive their bids, and can then respond through Guru's messaging system or take the conversation to your personal email or call.

Once you have reached an agreement with a provider, you can have them submit an invoice or escrow for the service, along with delivery dates that coincide with payment being released. Payment is secured using SafePay.

The big upside of Guru is that you can receive bids from different sources. Freelance individuals, as well as companies, will respond to your projects, and you can get a good idea of the going rate for the service you need.

There are two kinds of Guru freelancers. Free members don't pay a fee and can only bid on a few projects, these are particularly individuals with the most risk, but will likely have the lowest rates to finish your project.

There are also paid members who pay a small annual fee and can bid on a large number of projects. These are typically companies or very successful individuals that focus on a particular task and will have higher rates, and also have the feedback and references to back them up.

PeoplePerHour.com

PeoplePerHour is a UK based website that enables users to earn money online by advertising freelance opportunities for both Buyers and Sellers.

Building up a profile

Building up a profile simply means to build your profile in such a way that buyers can find you easily and offer you a job. To build a profile, you have to fill it up with all the details that you can gather related to your freelance career.

PeoplePerHour has a ranking algorithm that ranks your profile. The better the rank, the more chance you'll get for buyers to find your profile and offer you a job.

Propose Directly

PeoplePerHour.com also enables the Sellers to send direct proposals to Buyers on a job that is listed. To do that, you have to search for your relevant jobs on a daily basis and start sending proposals to the ones you think you can complete easily.

Hourlies

Hourlies is a special feature that PeoplePerHour.com has introduced for sellers. Hourlies are jobs that are posted by the sellers based on their skills.

Costs & Fees

With your free membership, you can bid on up to 15 jobs per month.In as much as it's not impossible to get started this way, most new freelancers will find that they need to bid on more than 15 jobs each week.

PeoplePerHour does enable you to purchase additional bids at the cost of $6.50 for just five bids.

How You Earn/Get Paid

PeoplePerHour.com pays sellers through a Paypal or Bank Account. To withdraw your earnings, you need to go to the Payment section and use the Withdraw Funds link.

Zirtual is a privately held American company that gives virtual assistant services to professionals, entrepreneurs and small corporate teams.

How It Works

Zirtual tasks typically fall into three main categories which include research, reservations, and scheduling. Their clients are majorly busy professionals who are in need of more free time, and as a "zirtual" assistant, you can provide that for them.

Payment

Virtual assistants are paid hourly by Zirtual.

Required Skills

- Prompt responses to clients' questions and requests.
- Internet savvy.
- Strong internet research skills and high-speed internet connection.
- Strong communication and problem-solving skills.
- Solid phone access; landline or dependable cell phone.
- Availability during working hours to respond to and engage with your clients.

- Familiarity with standard assistant tools like Google docs, Gcal, Microsoft Word, Excel and Outlook, etc.
- The company also advertises to their clients that all of the assistants are thoroughly screened and are college-educated. Hence, if you're not a college graduate, currently in college or at least have some college education, you may not be able to get on here.

Equipment

You need a computer, internet access, and a phone. Don't forget that some of the works you do will be scheduling appointments, reservations, booking flights, etc., so a phone line will probably be necessary for these purposes. Zirtual hires people from the U.S. only at this time. People from all states appear to be welcome to apply.

Summary

Freelance websites like: PeoplePerHour, Freelancer, Zirtual, Fiverr, and Guru, enables you to make money online without investing. For most, you can sign up and fill in the important details, and start sending proposals for jobs you are interested in.

All you need is your skills and internet. Most of the skills in demand are content writing, social media management, marketing, and website design.

If you have any of these, then you can sell your skill and make money online. These freelance platforms have policies that will protect you and potential employers.

CHAPTER TEN

EMAIL MARKETING

Email marketing is a powerful tool for acquiring, engaging, and retaining customers to help your business thrive. Email marketing occurs when a company sends a commercial message to a group of people by use of electronic mail.

Most commonly through advertisements, requests for business, or sales or donation solicitation. Any communication is considered email marketing if it helps to build customer loyalty, trust in a product or company or brand recognition.

Email marketing is an efficient way to stay connected with your clients while also promoting your business. With email marketing, you can easily and quickly reach target markets without the need for large quantities of print space, television/radio time or high production costs.

Thanks to effective email marketing software, you can maintain an email list that has been segmented based on several factors, including the length of time, addresses that have been on the list, customers' likes and dislikes, spending habits and other important criteria.

Emails are then created and sent out to specifically targeted members of your email list, providing them with a personalized detailed email information that they are interested in or have requested. This helps promote trust and loyalty to a company while also increasing sales.

Types of email marketing campaigns

- Email Newsletters: Email Newsletters are some of the most common and popular forms of email marketing. You can use email newsletters to give your subscribers with timely, expected, and helpful updates from your brand.

You can include how-to(s), announcements about your product or service, insider peeks into your business, or any other engaging content that adds value to your subscribers' inbox.

The rewards of email newsletters are increased retention and engagement, deepening of your relationships with subscribers, strengthening subscriber loyalty and their likelihood to recommend you.

- Acquisition Emails: Take full advantage of acquisition emails to drive trial and signups among those who have opted into your emails, but haven't converted. Send compelling offers or details to show them the value of becoming a paid or active customer.

Acquisition emails are a good way to grow your business, drive revenue, move leads through the conversion funnel faster, and focus your efforts on users who have expressed interest in what you give.

- Retention Emails: Retention emails is a powerful way to keep hard won users or customers active. Send a special message to subscribers who haven't opened an email from you lately, probably include a special offer or request feedback.

Strong retention emails help you increase retention and engagement, proactively reach out to at-risk users, and show customers you value their business.

- Promotional Emails: Create promotional emails to drive sales or signups, or to announce a new offering or special sale to entice your audience. Promotional offers are also a great way to encourage existing customers to try something new.

High-impact promotional emails are a great tool to reward engaged subscribers with special offers, drive new product or service adoption, and cross-sell existing products to your customer base.

Effective Email Marketing Steps

Email marketing campaigns can be a very powerful marketing tool. Marketers need to handle them with care. Therefore, here is an effective detailed step by step process for carrying out an effective email campaign.

Step 1: Emphasis on the Creation of Informative Content

Sending an email containg content that the target audience does not require will not grab the attention of the readers.

Step 2: Focus on Compatibility

An email that cannot reach the audience in the form it was meant will never be of much use. Therefore, marketers should focus on basic points about email compatibility.

Step 3: Segment the Target Audience

While it might sound easy to send a single email to all the people in a business email list, it is not advisable to do so. Emails are meant to be personal. Therefore, marketers should try and take advantage of this potential. Segmentation through email works just like any other form of segmentation.

Step 4: Use Tracking Tools

Once an email marketing campaign has been employed, the next step is to track the results. Tracking helps determine the effectiveness of the whole email marketing campaign. It helps an email marketing campaign become more effective in the long run.

How to Make Money with Email Marketing

Email marketing can be one of the most powerful ways to make money on the internet. Moreover, you must do it appropriately. Read on to discover how you can be the invited guest, and get the most from email marketing.

The Opting List

When people select the option to be included in your email list, that's called an Opt In. They are opting in to receive commercial messages from you. That means you've gotten their permission to send them offers.

This is important, because it protects you from being labelled a spammer. It strengthens the potential customer's likelihood of purchasing. Always start any email marketing campaign with a form that enables people to give you their email address. This is the foundation of list building.

The Message

Once you get someone to raise their hand and say, "Yes, tell me more. I'm interested in what you have to offer," you have opened them up to hearing your pitch. Make sure your offer is something they are interested in.

If you find that your email offers are converting well, then you'll be making money. On the other hand, you might not be so glad with the results. If not, use the list and give clients a survey. Ask the customers what they would like. It is crucial to craft your message and offer to be attractive to your list.

Repeated Communication

To make alot of money from your email list, you'll have to send repeated communications. An email is a busy form of communication. Your email may be sitting among 20 others and be neglected the first time.

To make repeated communications more successful, vary the message and subject. Moreover, keep the same offer. An auto responder can help out there. By setting up a series of timed emails to go to each person after they sign up, you can set the repeated communications on autopilot.

Testing

If you sign up for an email marketing service, you may be able to test different campaigns and see which one does better. While you may think one is better than the other, test results give you the truth. The most crucial thing to test is the headline in the subject of the email.

It is surprising how simple shifts in the subject line can allow your email to be opened before any others. Test them to discover which one gives you the best response.

This is an overview on how to make money through email marketing. Moreover, email is very difficult for your competitors to copy, because it's not openly published like a web page. Use this as the foundation for list building, and you will see more success using email.

CHAPTER ELEVEN

WEBINAR MARKETING

Webinar Marketing simply means promoting and testing your products to prospects and customers over the internet. The evidence is clear. Webinars are the fastest and easiest way to conduct business online, regardless of whatever niche you are in.

Webinar marketing is one of the best ways to build trust with your audience. This is powerful, because as you move your leads through the buyer's journey, trust is one of the biggest factors that will ascertain whether they will buy your products/services or your competitors.

Four Simple Steps for Creating Your Webinar

Webinars are one of the most effective communication tools of all time. Imagine creating your own webinar and showing your ideas, products, or services to a group of people at the same time! You are just a few simple steps away from maximum communication efficiency!

Step 1: Create a webinar presentation that gets people to take action

Every webinar must have a "call to action." This call to action could be "go to my website and buy my product", or it could be "pick up the phone and schedule an appointment" but the goal of every webinar is to make the webinar attendee to do something. Always remember this.

You'll have to create a webinar powerpoint presentation that entertains, informs, and has a clear call to action at the end. What do you want them to do?

Anyways, tell them precisely what to do and how to do it at the end of your webinar.

This is the first rule of webinar development.

Step 2: Pick a webinar hosting company

Choose a webinar hosting company that accommodates your needs and your budget. There are quite a few to select from. If you're looking forward to less than 1000 attendees and you plan on doing several webinars in a year, I suggest (GoToWebinar).

Step 3: Set up your webinar

After you have chosen a webinar host, you have to know how to set up the webinar. The webinar host will have a setup page that will ask you for a webinar title, description, date, and time. It will also ask you to set up any polls or surveys.

Polls are a great way to generate interaction with your attendees. A good poll question would be, "What is stopping you from achieving success in (your topic)." You would then show four obstacles and allow them to choose the most important obstacle to them.

This is a wonderful way to get your attendees to admit that they have an issue which has not yet been solved. When you show the results of the poll live on the webinar, it is a great social proof that they are not alone, and that many also struggle with this issue. They are also in a better place to seek for help by purchasing your products or services.

Step 4: Upload your registration web page

After you set up your webinar, you have to invite your attendees. You can use the generic registration page that the webinar hosting company gives you or you can create your own.

I prefer to create my own, so that I can control the look and feel of the registration page. This also enables me to differentiate myself from all the other webinars out there.

Reasons Why a Webinar is a Great Marketing Tool

- **Webinars are Convenient:** On-demand webinars are really convenient to have, due to at this point, everyone has an online connection and a means to access it.

Likely there are many of your business colleagues, partners, and customers have Internet access, as well. Conducting webinars enables you to connect with everyone around the world without them having to leave their home.

- **Webinars Can Create and Increase Brand Awareness:** Brand awareness is a concept that includes making the audience more aware of a brand or product through consistent promotion, advertisements, marketing, and labelling focused on a single theme, message, or identity.

Having a webinar set up will enable your audiences to have a visual image of your brand, resulting in a bigger consumer base when everything is said and done.

- **Webinars Establish Your Credibility:** By having a webinar, you will be able to give more reputation to your ideas. The simple act of putting on webinars will enable you, the people you're talking to, and the people who are watching, to comprehend your concepts and establish agreements.

You are presenting and sharing ideas in a forum of like-minded people, building upon them and even widening your viewpoints of the world around you.

- **Webinars Have Huge Applications on Training and Education:** Webinar live streams and webcasts can include how-to-do videos that showcase training in various fields of study and concepts. It is the kind of training that can be done online, broadcasted live and in real-time. It gives quick feedback from the viewer with questions through real-time comments.

- **Webinars Help Build a Bigger Audience and Contact List:** Just like with podcasts or simply having a YouTube channel, every webinar you make forges new contacts. Webinars enables you and other presenters to build an audience in the form of viewers, or even other people on your panel.

How to Make Money with Webinars

An increasingly popular idea in today's economy is to make money with Webinars. They are very powerful tools used to introduce new products, and build lists of followers for your business. If you are thinking about increasing sales, using webinars is a great idea.

- **Topic Selection:** You can run a webinar on just about anything. Moreover, you need to be fluent in the topic you pick. After all, you are advertising your business, so talk about things you know. Discuss about business, advertising, clients, network marketing, etc. Don't forget, this list is as limitless as your talents.

- **Promotion:** Once you decide on the topic, you will have to market it, so people will attend. I've seen the best webinars absolutely unattended due to inadequate marketing; Do not let this happen to you. The simplest way to do this is via social networking sites such as Twitter, Facebook or MySpace, your blog, and through email blasts. Another great way to promote is by posting on topic related forums.

- **Incentives:** One great way to ensure and increase your webinar attendance is to offer them something of value for attending. They should know it is free and they will only receive it at the end of the presentation.

- **The Presentation:** You want to keep the attention of your audience. If you choose a power point, ensure you use bullet points, graphs and statistics to hook their focus. Keep the delivery upbeat, energetic and engaging. Never use power point slides that have paragraphs. If you are using the teleseminar to introduce a new product or line, show them how much they need it!

- **Preparation:** Endeavour to prepare in advance what you will be saying. Note cards, prompts and practice is the rule. You don't want to appear to be groping around. You want to act and look as professional as you can while staying on task.

- **Finally:** After presenting, you'll want to give your webinar participants the opportunity to ask questions. Also, you'll want to exchange contact details, and probably you might want to give your business a plug. So by now, your audience will trust you, so don't come on too strong with the sales pitch. You want everyone to feel as if they received something for attending.

CHAPTER TWELVE

COPYWRITING

Copywriting is one of the basic skills that any person who wishes to be a great salesperson should endeavour to utilize in order to remain on top in the marketing industry.

It implies some basic elements that should come as no surprise: a mastery of the basic rules of grammar, vocabulary and a strong aptitude for making persuasive arguments.

There are more refined skills that distinguishes highly successful copywriters from the truly the mediocre ones. These include an understanding of the psychology of the demographic towards which the copy is directed, a clear knowledge of what the product offers that demographic and the ability to put that knowledge into words.

These skills requires time and more practice to develop to an excellent level.

Highly successful copywriters can really increase the success of their marketing efforts. The copy they create is always effective, does not need a commission when it makes a sale and it is one of the most cost-effective ways to increase market penetration for any product or service.

The skills required, moreover does not require money to develop and it takes nothing more than a word processor to create even the most complex and persuasive sales copy.

Contrast that with the software expenses needed to develop web pages and engage in other forms of marketing, it is readily apparent why this skill should be part of the fundamental toolbox used by anyone part of the sales or marketing.

Online, effective copy also comprises of elements of SEO which increases its visibility to those individuals who are looking for the product being advertised.

Intelligent copy that is well-written and reads easily is far more interesting when it comes up in search results than the mediocre, grammatically-incorrect varieties that tend to be so rampant on the Internet.

While the poor copy that so many individuals generate may be bad news for those who attempt to make sales based upon it, it is good news for those who take the time to develop the skills essential for generating truly excellent sales copy.

The following book will guide the reader through the fundamentals of generating effective advertising copy. A salesperson who takes the time to develop these skills can not only generate a great amount of sales through the effective use of their words, they can also save a great deal of money by avoiding the necessity of hiring a professional copywriter or copywriting service to handle their business on a contract basis.

These services can sometime be very expensive and may not produce exactly what the salesperson wants or the most effective possible copy for the product.

Additionally, the copywriting process helps to create an effective sales pitch that can be the basis for many other types of marketing. All that's needed to get started is literally a pen and a paper. In fact, this may be the best way to practice this necessary marketing skill.

While a typewriter or word processor may seem like a more convenient idea, the more intimate relationship provided by pen and paper is oftentimes more copacetic toward developing this skill than those methods.

The Copywriting Process:

Writing Great Headlines

The headline is the first pitch and, therefore, the first impression a reader will have regarding the product explained. Coming up with the right headline may take some time but the investment of time and effort is well worth it.

Before one even sets pen to paper, it's crucial to study other headlines. Research the market, get to know the target demographic and get into their heads. The headline should hit the reader with words that are powerful and enticing.

There are definitely some tried-and-true favorites where sales letter headlines are concerned. They include attention-grabbing words and phrases such as: Discover, The Amazing Secrets of..., Announcing, Introducing, Expose, Unlock, Unleash, Secrets, etc.

These words are all attention-grabbing and they show that something unknown and powerful is about to be explained. These words are frequently seen in sales letter headlines simply because they work.

The headline should address some key elements that have proven effective in garnering interest for the most successful marketers.

There are four principle elements that you should endeavor to achieve.
➢ Self-interest
➢ News
➢ Curiosity
➢ Quick and Easy

The first thing, self-interest, explains what the customer wants. Any customer wants to know why they should spend their hard-earned money on the product being offered.

This question can be reduced to "What's in it for me?" For instance, a headline that addresses the self-interest element might be along the lines of "How to Self-Publish Your Own Book and Make it a Best-Seller." Clearly, this heading implies that there is something in it for the reader and answers the question effectively and directly.

The news item means that the product's sales pitch should imply a sense of something new being announced. The product needs to be described as something that was not available before.

A news headline would imply that what is being advertised is a solution to a long-standing problem that has only been addressed with the advent of the product being pitched.

For instance: "Finally, an amazingly simple weight loss method that always works. Lose four or five pounds quickly, look healthier and happier than either with American's best weight loss secret, without diet, hard exercise or pills."

This headline communicates to the reader that what is being offered is both novel and noteworthy for being much different than what's been available in the past as far as weight loss programs go. Notice that the weight loss product headline is very long.

A headline need not be only a few words long. Sales copywriting, where headlines are concerned, is not bound by the same rules that govern headlines written for newspapers.

If a longer headline seems to constitute a better pitch, there's no reason to make it shorter impulsively.

A sales headline can even be two or three paragraphs long. Again, if the headline works better and sounds more enticing in a longer format, it's better to be effective than to be brief.

A curiosity headline oftentimes invokes the idea of a secret that holds the promise of generating something the reader wants. A good example of such a heading would be: "The only way left for the little guy to get rich. Here is the uncensored message that my wife asked me not to disclose."

This headline entices the reader by leaving a lot of open questions. How does the little guy get rich? What does the writer intend to convey against the objections of his wife? This sort of headline makes it almost impossible for the reader to not dedicate a bit of time toward reading the entire pitch.

The headline appeals to a reader's natural predisposition to favor those things which offer a quick and easy solution to a complex problem. Each of the above headlines implies that what's being sold will reward the reader for following through on the rest of the text by giving them something that will make their life easier and more convenient.

They also define a problem that vexes many people and which has yet to be availed of a solution that isn't overly-time consuming, painful or complicated.

It is generally a good idea to write the headline before writing the copy. It provides parameters for the persuasive argument that is to follow and defines the theme of the sales letter.

Do not be afraid to write several different headlines. It might take 100 headlines before the one that really makes the pitch sparkle comes along. This task is so vital to the usefulness and success of the sales copy that one should not be hesitant to dedicate a great deal of time toward the effort.

Once the right headline is written, it should jump off the page and make it essentially impossible for anyone who reads it to not develop an interest in hearing the rest of what's being said.

Writing the Copy

Great copywriting starts with the very first paragraph which, after the headline, is likely the part most responsible for gaining and retaining the reader's interest. The technique of having a strong first paragraph is essential to any form of writing, news, fiction, political speech and the rest of it.

This technique is equally important to sales writing. The idea is to pique your reader's interest and to draw them in to the rest of the text much as it was the goal with the headline but with the added advantage of having more space in which to accomplish this task. There are certain techniques that make the logistics of this effort easy to understand. A few are listed beneath.

- If/Then Statements: The if/then statement is a powerful persuasion technique and one of the foundational elements of successful copywriting. Examples of this would include.
- "If you are trying to make your lawn beautiful, then this is the most relevant message you will ever read."
- "If you're interested in beginning your own business but don't know where to begin, what follows will let you in on the secrets of the pros."

Notice how each of these statements resolves the same concerns that determine whether or not a headline is good. They define a challenge and a solution, they pique the reader's curiosity, they address the self-interest element common to everyone and they make the whole of affair of fulfilling these many needs seem very quick and easy: just read below.

Leads such as this are powerful at a visceral level and make it virtually impossible for the reader to look away once they have gotten this far.

The first sentence also presents an opportunity for the writer to take the rest of the paragraph in a direction that will enable them to convince the reader through more evidence and the skillful presentation of what the product has to offer.

The first sentence sets the tone for what's to follow and should always set up a scenario that lends the opener to being easily followed-up with strong and persuasive that make the rest of the pitch something that naturally follows and which doesn't sound forced.

Don't forget that a good sales letter should read in a way that never seems pasted together or scattershot.

Asking a Question

Asking customers, a question is a technique common to all successful sales. It isn't, moreover, quite as straightforward as one might believe. In this case, the copywriter walks sort of a tightrope. The question must be phrased in such a way that the answer is advantageous toward making the sale.

The question must also be necessarily restrictive, so that the reader's attention is directed where the writer intends. Do not ask broad yes or no questions.

Yes or no questions have the quality of making it very simple to inadvertently stop the sale by simply enabling the reader to make their determination regarding what is being sold very fast and, thus, raising the possibility that they'll lose interest as soon as they answer the question.

For instance, do not ask a question such as "Do you make mistakes in English?" There is the distinct possibility that the reader may make hardly any mistakes when writing and thus their answer would be "no".

Of course, this also means that they would likely have little interest in whatever product is being offered from that point on as the yes or no question has afforded them a means to determine that the product offers nothing they need.

Phrase questions in a broad way. "Do you make these mistakes in English?" would be preferable to simply "Do you make mistakes in English?"

The broader question makes it possible to keep the reader engaged a bit longer, at least long enough to offer a list of some common English mistakes and to possibly invoke one or two with which the reader does, indeed, have a bit of difficulty.

Keep the conversation open. An opening question is intended to pique the reader's interest and to make what is written seem relevant to them. Open-ended questions makes it obvious that they can't simply read the one interrogative, decide that it doesn't apply and leave reading the rest of the sales letter.

Benefits And Features

The first paragraph is generally a place where the writer tells their story. This means answering the question and then describing how they discovered the solution. For instance, if one were marketing a weight loss product, they might open with the shocker, ask the question and then proceed to tell the story about how they discovered the weight loss program being explained.

Benefits and features are two separate things entirely. To comprehend the difference, it is important to comprehend how these items are listed within effective sales copy. Benefits answer the questions posed to the reader.

Most essentially, they answer the "What's in it for you?" element of the sales pitch. Bullet points are a good way to address the need to answer such questions.

For instance:

How will the weight loss program improve the quality of my life?

➢ No working out
➢ No gym fees
➢ No pills

This rhythm of asking the question and answering by way of listing benefits is very effective and gives the reader the sense that their needs can be met by buying the product. Notice that all of these statements are concise and that they don't beg a question. This is what defines them as features.

To find out whether or not a statement explains a reward or a feature, one may use a very simple criterion.

A feature is something that invites the reader to ask "so what?" For instance, "Our gym is open 24 hours per day," is a feature. So, what if the gym is open 24 hours per day?

What does that mean to the reader? It may or may not be interesting to them and presents to them the opportunity to simply say it is not useful to them and they would be better off spending their money somewhere else.

A reward, moreover, takes the feature and gives it a context. "Our gym is open 24 hours per day so that our clients can work out anytime they want!" The statement is now a benefit as it has a clearly defined end to the question.

If the reader can read and statement as say "So what?", it's a feature. If they cannot ask that question after having read the statement, then it is a feature.

This simple formula can help the writer use benefits and features to their most persuasive effect and stop them from asking questions that may result in the customer simply dismissing the feature being offered as something that does not resolve their needs.

Testimonials

Testimonials are majorly used in sales copy that they merit their own section. Eventough they are used, they are often used to poor effect and even abused. Testimonials are a resource, not a filler material to make up for poor copywriting.

They can be really effective provided a few simple rules are followed. Testimonials should never open a sales letter. They should follow the second paragraph, at the earliest. They are a tool for helping to relate the narrative relevant to the product but that narrative must be told first.

Testimonials should follow the listing of the benefits. The testimonials cement the sales letter by offering evidence that the reader can trust the writer.

The writer has already gained the reader's interest, listed the benefits to their products and the testimonials give the reader an expectation of what sort of results they can expect from doing business with the writer.

Testimonials that appear at the beginning of the document have no context which makes them not at all understandable. Without the narrative provided by the copy, they stand out in the open air, defining nothing that the reader has yet been made to comprehend.

Testimonials depicts results, success and the trustworthiness of the copywriter. You have to use them as reinforcement, not as a means for stating their first case.

Backing it Up

The reader is going to want a bit of assurance before they part with their money. This means the salesperson has to put themselves on the line so that the reader can trust them without feeling like a fool for having done so. This oftentimes entails making a guarantee of one sort or another.

It's a general rule that a longer guarantee is preferable to a shorter one, for obvious reasons. A 60-day guarantee is better than a 30-day guarantee and a 90-day guarantee is preferable to either. Of course, a year-long guarantee would be better than a 90-day guarantee.

Don't forget that a guarantee has to have an element of specificity to be worthwhile to the customer. "Satisfaction Guaranteed!" appears on a multitude of advertisements.

It means completely nothing. Never use this guarantee. It's hard to attest that anyone will be satisfied with a product and it should be removed completely from sales copy.

An Offer they can't Ignore

Now that the reader is interested in the product and they've been informed of its features and benefits, assured of its quality and heard from other customers who have had great results from using it, it's time to give them something back for their time.

This means making an offer. The offer should be so powerful that they couldn't pass it up without feeling a bit silly for having doing so. One way to make such an offer is to engulf the customers.

This usually entails offering deals that comes at savings which are legitimate but which hit the customer as being almost hard to believe. Some instances of an overwhelming value include: "Right now you can get $500 worth of bonuses for only $97!"

A part of this technique is called comparing apples to oranges. It's simple and effective and works in the following manner.

"The seminar costs $3,000 but this home study course not only includes every minute of the material reviewed at the seminar, but also includes the Question and Answers section.

If you buy today it's only $697. Plus, you will exclude the need to travel and to stay at a hotel, which can save substantial amounts of money. Of course, you listen to the seminar as many times as you want."

In this case, the comparison is made between the two options presented for obtaining the details from the seminar. Attending the seminar is characterized as expensive and time-consuming while simply purchasing the home study kit is revealed as economical and time-saving.

The fact that the home study kit can be used as often as desired is also emphasized, which defines another reward for the consumer. It's not an overstatement to say that one should really try to make the customer feel stupid if they do not act on the offer.

The rewards, price and guarantee should define an opportunity that no rational person would pass up easily. Convenience-based pitches are particularly effective toward this end. Why would the consumer not want to have the seminar materials on-hand when the only other option is to attend the seminar live and all the expenses that is required?

Now that all of that work has been done, the most frequently overlooked and incorrectly-executed element of the sales letter comes into play: Telling the reader how they help themselves with the product.

How do they get it?

In far too many cases, an excellent sales letter, at the end, leaves the customer absolutely confused as to how they actually go about getting the product they have been pitched. This is one of the most critical parts of copywriting and constitutes the element of sales writing where the greatest number of errors are made.

This requires a distinct and clear call to action being presented to the customer. There should be no mystery as to how they place their order and the more distinct the means describe the better; for the salesperson and the customer alike.

Deliver the details in the same direct and clear fashion as one might expect an ER surgeon to give instructions to their staff or a military commander would direct their troops. Simple, comprehensive and clear statements.

Don't say "Call Now!" Say "Call 1-800-555-4216 and tell the operator to place your order for Product Y." Don't say "Send your order today!"

Say "Fax your completed order form, including billing information, to 1-800-555-1313. Be sure to include a non-PO box address for delivery." These statements are basically commands and have the effect of giving the customer all the details they need to complete the order in a clear, concise statement.

A call to action should be followed by the instilling a sense of urgency into the whole affair. This requires specific considerations which are detailed beneath.

Why should they do it now?

Instilling a sense of urgency into the sale is so important that it merits its own section. Quite often, this task is accomplished by making an offer that has a definite expiration date.

An instance would be "Respond within 40 days and get 6% off!" This gives the customer a reason to act sooner rather than later. It also increases the element of making the offer they can't refuse.

Another instance would be making an offer based upon rewarding the first Y number of clients. For instance: "This offer is only available to the first 90 customers."

Time-limited offers not only add a sense of urgency, they present a reward for acting instantly. When offering these soft of pitches, it is crucial to keep honest in mind.

The idea is to create urgency while still conveying that what is being sold is valuable and useful to the customer. This plays into the news aspect of sales writing.

A product may be available on a free trial basis because it is a new product on the market or a remarkably improved version of an already-existing product. It may be offered at a discount because a large amount of stock is available but not because there is not a demand for the product.

Let the customers know that they only have a limited time to get in on the deal being offered, but make certain they have enough time to make the decision without feeling like they're being hurried.

For instance, a 5-day special offer is only useful for a week and will seem as if it were contrived if it is extended for another week immediately afterwards.

A 20-day special offer is manageable, enables a customer to consider the purchase and still has enough of a time limit that it needs initiative and can increase the amount of sales while it is active.

- **Don't Ever Lie**

After all that work put into gaining a customer's confidence, it would be a shame to tear it all down by telling a lie. A lie might not be intentional. If an offer is given on a time-limited basis, any materials related to that offer must be updated in accordance with the expiration of the offer.

For example, if a webpage offers an enticement to the first 100 customers, it should be revised as soon as the first 100 customers have placed their orders.

This has to do with the single greatest asset any salesperson has: credibility. If the customer cannot believe the salesperson's word, how can they have any justified faith in the product itself? There are some ways to word these offers which insulate the salesperson from putting their claims to the lie.

Free trials are a good example of how one makes these accommodations to protect their credibility. If a salesperson has an offer that cannot be kept going forever while still generating a reasonable profit, it makes sense to use qualifiers that ensure that they're not over-promising.

Closed, committal statements versus more open-ended, unmanageable statements can be described as follows: "Customers will get free resale rights to this book!" versus "The first 30 customers will get free resale rights to this book." "Free trial version available!" versus "Limited quantities of free trial versions are available."

In both instances, the latter statements are safe and the former statements too broad and at risk of becoming lies. Should a customer call in and ask for a free trial version based upon the first statement and find out that there are no more free-trial versions available, they are likely to feel as if they have been deceived.

In the second statement, they can simply be told that the free trial versions have all been distributed already. In that latter instance, they have not been lied to and they won't feel they have been deceived, they'll simply be made aware that they acted too late to take advantage of the offer.

The significance of honesty is certainly vital to comprehend. A client who feels that they've been deceived will likely view the salesperson as a fraud.

While the salesperson may be neither and simply be a victim of their own carelessness, the reputation will likely be long-lasting and difficult to correct. Surely, the salesperson can expect no further business from that jilted customer.

It is also an opportunity to make the letter more personal. The salesperson should attach their name to the sales letter at this point.

Adding one's name to an offer is to add a touch of personal honor to the whole stuff; the equivalent of giving one's word that what is being sold is worth the money and that the value of any special offers are so good that the salesperson does not stop to associate themselves personally with them.

Don't forget that there's been a guarantee offered.

● **Walking Through an Open Door**

Buying a product is always accompanied by a positive emotional response. The client clearly feels as if they have done well for themselves, getting a product that offers something that will relief some sort of pain they are feeling and replace it with the joy that comes with having that pain resolved.

In fact, some psychologists theorize that these are the two fundamental psychological motivators in human beings: Increasing pleasure and decreasing pain. Once the client is in a buying state of mind, it makes sense to take advantage of that by offering them more. Make certain that, at the end of the copy, they're offered another opportunity. This is called upselling and is a basic sales skill.

Consider the situation if one calls into a home shopping service that operates via infomercials. As soon as the client announces to the operator that they would like to purchase a given product, they are made aware that there are other products that naturally go along with their intended purchase.

They may also be offered an extended warranty or some other bonus for their challenges. In some cases, it's actually hard to simply make the original purchase because of all that's being offered in this manner.

The last part of the sales letter should offer a similar service. Throw in a few bonuses for a little extra money. Offer additional products that go along with the ones being offered or make a convincing segue into another product entirely.

When a client already has their credit card out, they are ready to buy and will be easily persuaded to spend a bit more if they're being offered something valuable.

This is not exploiting a state of mind but simply addressing the customer's desire to have their most fundamental needs met at the time when they are present in their mind to a great degree.

Never give up this opportunity. After the client has been convinced, it makes sense to ratchet up the sales a bit. Upselling is an incredibly important sales technique and is much more easily done than is making a sale from scratch.

A good sales letter consist the following:
◆ A strong, attention-grabbing headline.
◆ An opening paragraph that holds their interest.
◆ Bullet points that explains features and benefits.
◆ Testimonials that remove skepticism.
◆ Guarantees that secures trust.
◆ An offer they cannot refuse.
◆ Particular instructions regarding how to order.
◆ A closing with a sense of urgency.
◆ A P.S. that maximizes response

SECTION 4

Additional Tips to Consider

CHAPTER THIRTEEN

DO'S TO APPLY

Most businesses understand that content is a crucial part of their online marketing success, but not all businesses know how to use their content very well to get the most profitable effect.

The issue is further complicated by the fact that there's a lot of outdated or bad advice going around. It isn't always easy to know which bits can be trusted.

Fortunately, I've sorted out the wheat from the chaff for you.Here are the things you must do if you plan to be successful with online marketing.

◆ **Always invest in building your online presence**

Guess what takes place when an employer in the digital industry searches for your name on Google and sees nothing? If you don't have profiles built and optimized for LinkedIn, Twitter, etc., or even a personal blog or website to display who you are and what you stand for, people are going to question your commitment to digital and social media.

Anytime you say you are passionate about digital – don't just pay it lip service, show it by getting active in it.

◆ **Always identify with your Audience**

This is the first and most crucial step to take. You have to comprehend what the interests of your customers are, and what they are most likely to type into a search engine when searching for the type of service you offer.

This will enable you to target your marketing strategy directly to the people who are willing to commit to purchasing, signing up for or contacting you straight on.

There are various excellent online tools that can aid you in making your marketing strategy much more effective. You can use the basic tools that Google offers to find out what people search for most, and which keywords don't have a lot of strong competition, so that you won't have to fight for a good position in SERPs.

◆ **Where you could reach your Clients**

Alot of people use social media fairly regularly in our today's world, which makes this the perfect place to search for customers. Nevertheless, it is very crucial to be present on several different social media platforms.

This will help you promote your website in different ways, from sharing blog posts on Twitter, Facebook and LinkedIn to pinning pictures on Pinterest, and posting videos on YouTube and engaging fans in the comments.

This also depends on the product/service you are offering. For instance, if you are running an online clothing store, it is much better to reach out to your audience on websites such as Instagram and Pinterest than on Facebook.

This is a very crucial thing to research and experiment with. The best way is to test multiple social media sites and analyze the data you've acquired. This will give you a lucid picture of where you can reach the majority of your customers.

◆ **How do you find that Audience?**

Begin by figuring out the problem your product or service solves. Next, list the characteristics of an average customer to pinpoint your target market. It's also crucial to know who makes up your primary audience.

They are the ones who need your product or service the most. For instance, if your business specializes in home security systems, your primary customer may live in a residential area with a high crime rate.

◆ **Always Fit Your Content into a Cohesive Marketing Strategy**

Great content scattered all over the place will have some effect. You'll likely have some sparkling successes, but you'll also have your fair share of mediocrity too.

When you have a unique marketing strategy in place, and know actually what you want to get, you'll find it easy to align your content with your business goals. That way, everything will be working towards a common ideal, and you will have a much greater chance of achieving it.

◆ **Take steps to increase web traffic to your site**

The Internet has become a very competitive place for business owners. The competition is much, and it's every business for itself.

In cyberspace, content is king. Utilize it to entice potential customers to visit your site. Make it simple for visitors to share their experiences on Facebook, Twitter, Reddit and other social media sites.

Adding an irresistible offer and a call to action on each page can also drive web traffic.Ensure your visitors know exactly what it is you want them to do. It could be signing up for an e-newsletter or a free 15-minute consultation.

Offering something that relates to your business and appeals to your target market is another way to increase web traffic. It can be a free ebook, white paper or anything that's been precisely written for your target customer.

◆ **Always Analyze**

The best thing about online marketing is that you can take advantage of numerous online tools to get incredibly accurate data about the effects of your campaign. You can easily check how much time users spend on your website and how many of them make a purchase.

Based on this data, you can easily adjust your website and your marketing campaign, to make them more effective. A detailed analysis should follow every single change you make.
These online marketing tips are going to make your business blossom.

Moreover, you can always turn to sponsored posts on other blogs, ad campaigns and other available forms of paid advertising. In as much as it takes a little bit of investment, by following detailed

information about your marketing campaign, you can maximize your ROI. The choice is yours.

Whatever you decide to go for, pay attention to the little details, and you are surely going to make your business.

◆ Always Boost your website ranking

Search engines continue to drive the majority of visitors to websites. That's why it's crucial to have a website that is search engine friendly. Also, every page should be optimized and designed for mobile search.

Keywords and keyword phrases also play a critical role in boosting your website ranking. Keywords are what someone types into a search engine, such as Google, Yahoo Search, Ask or Bing, when they're "searching" for something.

Generate a list of keywords or phrases people might use to find your website.

Take advantage of tools, like the Google Keyword Tool, to get an idea of the most searched phrases. Integrate several of them throughout your website in titles, content, even rename your images to contain the keywords or phrase.

Another way to boost your website ranking is by adding captions to your pictures and images that incorporate your keywords. Add an ALT tag to explain the image. Don't forget to add the same keyword phrase in the text near the image.

Search engines want to be sure users have access to the most up-to-date details. Ensure your website content is regularly updated. This tells search engines that your site is ever-changing and current.

Believe it or not, Internet marketing is here to stay. In the future, it will become an even greater force when it comes to how businesses operate.

Whether you're new to online marketing or a seasoned professional, implementing these strategies can aid you break down barriers and use this modern communication tool for your advantage.

Don't to Avoid

When it comes to marketing, success comes from knowing what not to do, as well as knowing what you should do. In our world today, there are many online marketing opportunities, most of which are self-service. While that's convenient, it can make it too simple for a company to get an advertising campaign up and running.

In fact, it might be so simple that a company doesn't take the time to think things through, and ends up making a serious marketing mistake that can badly affect a campaign altogether.

Below are online marketing mistakes you should try to avoid:

◆ Thinking Pre-Internet Marketing Simply Needs to Be Moved Online

One of the major mistakes people make is thinking successful online marketing doesn't just mean taking what worked before the internet and moving it online. The truth is, people act differently with the internet and mobile devices than they did with old media.

Potential customers have more control, choices, and details than ever, and what worked when print and television were dominant can't just be moved online and expected to perform.

Successful digital marketing must be important, and it must reach the people it's important to. Attaining this needs smart use of marketing data and an internet-age technique to marketing.

◆ **Don't Fail to Develop a Plan to Monitor the Marketing Campaign**

It's not unusual for a business owner to create a wonderful marketing plan that has all of the bells and whistles on it. From designing an innovative social media campaign to making sure the website has been well optimized for the major search engines, a lot of work goes into the first planning.

In as much as the marketing campaign has been well thought out for deployment, the owner may not see the need for following through with a plan to monitor the marketing campaign on an ongoing basis. Which means, the success of the overall campaign may be compromised needlessly.

To avoid these issues, the business owner and their representatives should create a solid plan that will monitor the campaign's success from the initial start-up. This ongoing plan is designed to figure out and pinpoint areas that may need to be changed.

Specifically, the opportunities that have the capability for capturing a larger target audience. For instance, the business owner may need to spend a little bit more money to get the maximum benefits in their social marketing strategy.

Simply stated, with only an additional small investment, the campaign may draw in more visitors from LinkedIn, Facebook, and Twitter.

◆ **Don't Exclude Tools that Provide Measurable Data**

Another mistake that business owners can avoid is excluding tools that can provide the business with essential measurable data.

Fortunately, there is a lot of great information online, along with valuable tools to develop, launch and monitor a marketing campaign for virtually any business venture.

These marketing tools can be used for many different purposes, and they are needed to see how the marketing campaign is performing.

Some of the most crucial tools are being provided by third party vendors, as well as by major players like Google. These tools are available to give the business owners and their marketing specialists specific information about how many visitors access the site, as well as how long these visitors remain on the site looking around.

Based on the complexity of the tools, the site owner will have an opportunity to see if the sales for their products have changed dramatically since the marketing campaign was deployed.

◆   **Don't fail to choose a unique brand name.**

You need a truly unique brand to match your ambitious projections. Be sure to research the market, so that you are certain no one else already has your brand name, and check that a suitable.com domain is available.

Even the biggest companies can make the mistake of not having done enough market research for a unique brand name. Having something unique would get people interested.

◆   **Don't fail to have a backup plan**

It is very common for people, even business owners, to undervalue their data. "It won't happen to me," you may think. Though you may be able to avoid a fire or a flood, what about a Trojan that remotely infects your files, one by one until you can no longer access your data?

You are more vulnerable than you think -- even huge international companies have their mishaps so, always have a backup solution in place for these inevitable situations.

◆ Don't ail to proofread your copy

Don't underestimate the importance of proofreading everything before you publish it. Don't think that it is up to the web developer to pick up on errors.

It is vital that you remove all typos and grammatical errors, so that your text is readable and free-flowing. You can improve your grammar by using a range of easily accessible online tools and grammar guides.

◆ Don't Alienate Search Engines

Almost everyone comprehends the value of search engine optimization, but many websites remain woefully inept at utilizing all of the SEO tools available for efficient and effective optimization.

For instance, a site that prioritizes the company name is less likely to achieve search engine ranking as high as a site that focuses on more generic terms.

The more specific you are in your SEO keywords, the more precise the search terms will need to be to point toward your site.

Focus on a general stable of keywords that deal broadly with your company's services. This way, you will be able to appear before potential customers that may not comprehend the most specific aspects of your business. Rely on your site's content to handle the specifics.

◆ Don't Ignore Analytics

Analytics is an area that usually causes anxiety among business owners. Many business owners assume analytics is an overly complicated area and choose to ignore the valuable data that can be referenced and acted upon.

Analytics is simply a measure of your Internet marketing campaign's effectiveness. Resources are finite and time can be stretched, therefore analytics help you to view the progress of your various Internet marketing endeavours and give you the opportunity to direct your energy toward those areas that bear the most fruit.

◆ Don't Target the Wrong Audience

This is one of the biggest mistake in the marketing Industry. Marketing is not only about spreading the product around the world. A perfect marketer is one who makes a deep research about the product, including research of its reach.

Have you ever asked yourself why big brands like Apple, Microsoft, Facebook, etc., are so successful? I know we never think about it, but let me tell you, they have a complete plan. They know their audience.

They have a perfect team who just check the strong demographic conventions. That's why those brands rocket into the sky faster and are leading the world. Marketing is not just about getting featured in magazines, top sites, and publications. It consists of a certain life cycle. Just like a System Development Life Cycle, marketing works the same.

If you want to make your marketing campaign successful, then you must take a look at your audience. The selection of the wrong audience will lead you towards failure.

CHAPTER FOURTEEN

PREMIUM TOOLS AND SERVICES TO CONSIDER

Online Marketing Tools refers to any online software or portal that you can use to create, build, manage and promote an online business within the Internet marketing arena.

It is true to say that almost every job completed by any piece of software could be done by hand. The software is typically designed to automate the process, and save considerable time for the user.

Any of these premium online marketing tools that can aid you in skyrocketing your online money making.

Social Media Tools

◆ **Buffer**

Buffer is a social media management tool that will help you streamline your social posting efforts. We already know how powerful social media is for your marketing initiatives, but leveraging a tool like Buffer will help you increase your followers, engage your audience, and build your brand.

The benefit of Buffer is its ability to let you connect multiple accounts to one dashboard. Buffer's free plan is perfect for new businesses looking to grow their social presence. To unleash the full power of the software, you might want to consider one of their upgraded plans.

HootSuite is a wonderful tool. You can use the scheduler to pre-schedule your posts for a specific date and time, and you can preview how it will look.

Using HootSuite's "streams," you can view all of your posts on all of your networks in a visual format, which makes it very easy to keep track of what you are posting and where.

You can also track your campaigns analytics; a handy feature for those who are always reporting the success of their social media campaigns.

File Management Tools

Dropbox

Dropbox is now top in demand tool for businesses, due to it makes sharing documents with others very easy. This personalized, cloud-based tool improves productivity, since you can share folders in real-time, which helps collaboration among team members so simple.

Dropbox makes available a free basic plan that features 2GB of space. If you have more space, you'll have to update either to the Pro ($9.99) or Business plans ($15).

Organizational Tools

Evernote

Actually, there's no more popular tool for online marketers than Evernote. Whether it's researching notes, resources, or to-do lists, Evernote makes the research and outline process of content writing a breeze.

Whether it's writing down notes for a business presentation or collaborating with a project with team members, Evernote replaces the endless amounts of paper that used to fill up your desk.

Evernote can be gotten on any device, so you can work on your projects while at the airport, and then complete them when you get back home to your laptop. Plus, I didn't even mention the neat dictation feature either.

Grammarly

Grammarly is your free writing app that ensures everything you type is easy to read, effective, and mistake-free. As you type, Grammarly will underline any spelling or grammatical errors and help you fix them on the fly.

Human editors are great. Built-in spellcheckers are nice. However, neither are perfect. It's good to add another layer of editing to your writing and Grammarly is the answer. This powerful tool automatically checks anything you write or publish in an Internet browser.

Email Marketing Tools

Mailchimp

Email marketing is imperative to the success of most businesses. While building a brand on platforms like YouTube, Facebook, Instagram and Twitter are important, you're limited to the constraints of those channels.

This makes it particularly difficult to move consumers through a funnel, and provides you with relatively little control.

However, email provides a more intimate interaction between a brand and consumers by offering you the tools you need to effectively nurture leads. Mailchimp is an excellent free email marketing tool and one of the easiest for newbies to learn.

SEO Tools

Google Trends

Google Trends
Google Trends is another neat Google product. This free tool enables you to search for keywords based on volume, and identify the potential of different short and long-tail search terms.

Moz

Moz is another SEO tool that's super easy to use and navigate. You can see how your keywords are ranking, compare keywords side-by-side to see how they compare against one another and see which search engines are sending traffic to your site right from your dashboard.

Keyword tool.io

Keywords are the major cornerstones of every SEO or marketing campaign. Use Keyword tool.io to see a list of useful and important long-tail keywords that may be useful to assist target customers.

Analytics and Optimization Tools

Google Analytics

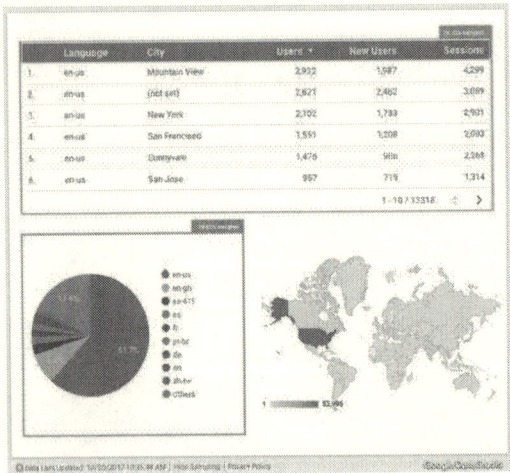

Google Analytics is one of the best tools for monitoring the results of your website traffic and where that traffic comes from. The graph view is particularly handy to visually see when your website traffic goes up and down, so you can better comprehend how to capitalize on the actions that caused traffic to increase.

With Google Analytics URL Builder, you can create unique links for individual influencers. This gives you a simple way of tracking social media efforts and tying them to revenue. It's an easy-to-use tool with many benefits under the surface.

Visual Content Tools

Piktochart

Piktochart is a wonderful little program that allows you to create graphic design-worthy infographics. It's pretty user friendly, and you don't have to be a designer to end up with a beautiful infographic.

It stores all of them in your account, so you can edit them at any time. That is great for those clients who need 60,000 changes.

Prezi

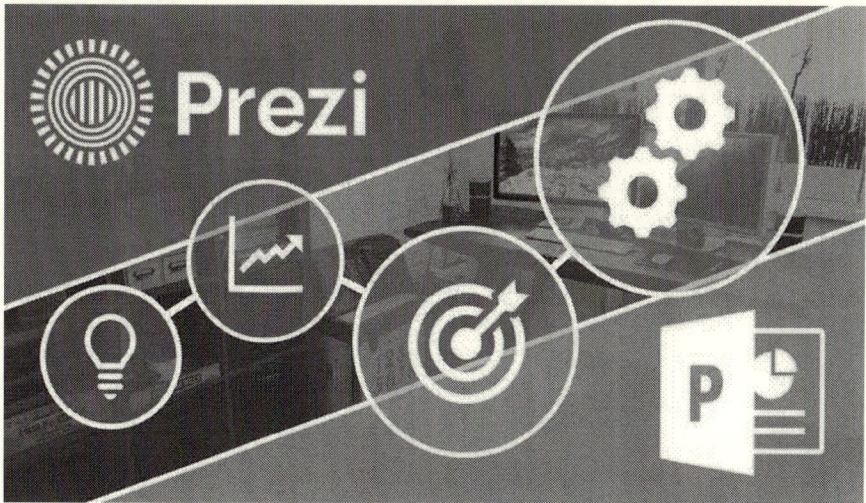

Prezi is another wonderful way to create visual content easily. Prezi is a super cool presentation application that runs on the cloud. If you want to create out-of-the-box content that shows information in a compelling and interesting way, try Prezi.

Canva

Obviously, not everybody can pay to hire a graphic designer, but nearly all of us can learn to do some basic design by ourselves. Canva makes design easy and fast. Its tagline, "Amazingly simple graphic design software," is great.

Canvas templates are optimized for social media, and they are great. With just a few customizing clicks, you're all set with great visual content.

Canva doesn't charge a dim to use the cloud-based software. If you use "premium elements" you can pay as you go. CanvaForWork is an advanced feature of the tool that charges a monthly subscription of $12.95.

SurveyMonkey

SurveyMonkey is one of the most popular free online premium survey tools. Surveys are a good way to collect consumer information, engage customers, uncover trends and secure tangible insights on your business.

SurveyMonkey is a well-known free online premium survey tools. Surveys are a good way to collect consumer details, engage customers, uncover trends and secure tangible insights on your business.

SurveyMonkey's software is really easy. In just minutes, you can design, create and publish your business survey. Furthermore, you'll be able to check the results in the backend.

REFERENCES

1.http://mashable.com/2007/07/30/make-money-online/#v31pl6YIl5qc(accessed on 1st June ,2020).

2.http://www.johnchow.com/12-free-tools-to-make-money-online/(accessed on 2nd June ,2020).

3.http://www.ivetriedthat.com/2013/03/18/how-to-create-and-make-money-from-your-own-online-course/(accessed on 4th June, 2020).

4.http://blog.teachable.com/best-ways-to-make-money-from-home-online-2016(accessed on 1st June ,2020).

5. http://basicblogtips.com/blogging-to-make-money.html(accessed on 21st June ,2020).

6. http://www.loudtips.com/true-facts-blogging-really/(accessed on 1st June ,2020).

7. https://earnforum.net/(accessed on 5th June ,2020).

8.   http://www.emoneyspace.com/forum/(accessed   on   5th June ,2020).

9.https://www.shoutmeloud.com/best-recurring-affiliate-program.html(accessed on 4th June ,2020).

10.https://theblogpress.com/blog/how-to-make-money-online-with-affiliate-programs-video/(accessed on 5th June ,2020).

11. https://mixergy.com/webinars-to-drive-sales/(accessed on 3rd June ,2020).

12. https://www.youtube.com/watch?v=LTCY8nWTU(acaccessed on 1st June ,2020).

13.http://www.lifehack.org/articles/money/10-scam-free-ways-make-money-online-inforgraphic.html(accessed on 10th une ,2020).

14.http://howtomakemoneyfromhome411.com/wp-content/uploads/2015/04/how-to-make-money-from-home-infographic-2.jpg/(accessed on 5th June ,2020).

15. http://20smoney.com/case-studies/(accessed on 11th June ,2020).
16. http://howtomakehonestmoneyonline.com/case-studies(accessed on 12th June ,2020).

17.http://www.myonlinebizjourney.com/people-who-make-money-online/accessed on 13th June ,2020).

18.http://www.ogbongeblog.com/2012/07/12-making-money-online-facts-you-must.html(accessed on 15th June ,2020).

Stephen Akintayo, (Africa Most Sought-after Investment Coach) an inspirational speaker and Serial Entrepreneur is currently the Chief Executive Officer of Stephen Akintayo Consulting International and Gtext Media and Investment Limited, a leading firm in Nigeria whose services span from Digital Marketing, Website Design, Bulk SMS, Online Advertising, Media, E-Commerce, Real Estate, Consulting and a host of other services.

Stephen, Also Founded GileadBalm Group Services which has assisted a number of businesses in Nigeria to move to enviable levels by helping them reach their clients through its enormous nationwide data base of real phone numbers and email addresses.

It has hundreds of organizations as its clients including multinational companies like Guarantee Trust Bank, PZ Cussons, MTN, Chivita, among others.

Stephen, popularly called Pastor Stephen is also the founder of Omonaija, an online radio station and SAtv in Lagos currently streaming for 24 hours daily with the capacity to reach every country of the world.

To invite Stephen Akintayo for a speaking engagement kindly visit stephenakintayo.com email: info@stephenakintayo.com or call: 08180000618.

Made in the USA
Middletown, DE
09 January 2026

24681579R00080